Terrorism and the Law

Yonah Alexander

and

Edgar H. Brenner

Editors

Transnational Publishers, Inc.

Published and distributed by Transnational Publishers, Inc.
410 Saw Mill River Road
Ardsley, NY 10502, USA

Phone: 914-693-5100
Fax: 914-693-4430
E-mail: info@transnationalpubs.com
Web: www.transnationalpubs.com

Library of Congress Cataloging-in-Publication Data

Terrorism and the law / Yonah Alexander and Edgar H. Brenner, editors.
    p.cm.
  ISBN 1-57105-243-7
  1. Terrorism—United States. 2. Terrorism—United States—Cases. 3. Terrorism.
4. Terrorism—Cases. I. Alexander. II. Brenner, Edgar H.

KF9430 .T47 2001
345.73'02—dc21   2001036785

Manufactured in the United States of America

Contents

International Conventions, Declarations, U.N. Resolutions

Preface

The vulnerability of modern society and its infrastructure, coupled with the opportunities for the utilization of sophisticated high-level conventional and mass destruction weaponry, requires nations, both unilaterally and in concert to develop credible response strategies and capabilities to minimize future threats. The stunning success of terrorist bombings, kidnappings, hijackings, facility attacks, and assassinations has resulted in a popular awareness of the important counterterrorism measures that states apply. After all, state possess enormous legal, economic, police, and military resources that terrorists cannot match. Governments have taken domestic and international measures to deal with conventional acts of terrorism, and they have taken special precautions to deal with mass destruction threats.

Since it is generally easier to take steps at home than it is to promote international action, states have taken a wide variety of domestic measures. Most notably, they have given official attention to terrorism; notably improved intelligence-gathering resources against terrorists; the enactment of appropriate legislation; the apprehension, prosecution, and punishment of terrorists. They have provided improved protection to government facilities and government officials. Moreover, significant counterterrorist measures have been taken at airports where terrorists have been able to do great damage.

The legal response to terrorism is often misunderstood and not fully appreciated as an effective tool to combat terrorism. For example, some statutory loopholes in domestic law have been closed, as the experience of the United State suggests. A case in point is Congressional enactment of a "long arm" statute making it a federal crime for a terrorist to threaten, detain, seize, injure, or kill an American citizen abroad. Thus, the FBI in a sting operation in international waters off the coast of Cyprus arrested Fawaz Younis, a Lebanese operative in the 1985 hijacking of a Jordanian airline which had on board Americans who became hostages. Younis was taken to the United States and subsequently convicted and sentenced. In 1995, Ramzi Yousef, a conspirator in the 1993 World Trade Center bombing, was arrested in Pakistan and extradited to the United States. He was sentenced to life in prison.

The purpose of this book is to provide sample sources and court cases on the legal responses to terrorism both nationally and internationally. Part

I consists of presentations by academics, practitioners, and government officials on selected topics such as definitions, case studies, and intergovernmental policies and actions. The second part of the volume provides selected documents including state and federal laws of the United States, several domestic and international court cases, and a number of conventions and resolutions.

This book, which represents the fourth research effort in the Terrorism Library Series of Transnational Publishers, draws on materials generated over the past several years from dozens of international seminars and conferences, as well as fieldwork around the world. A previous work in this area is our four-volume set *Legal Aspects of Terrorism in the United States* (Oceana Publications, 2000). Other research studies are being planned for the future, including legislation and court cases in the United Kingdom, India, and elsewhere.

We wish to thank the Smith Richardson Foundation, the Stella and Charles Guttman Foundation, the Inter-University Center for Legal Studies (International Law Institute), the Inter-University Center for Terrorism Studies, and the International Center for Terrorism Studies (Potomac Institute for Policy Studies), for their support of our academic research on this important topic of public concern. Neither of the aforementioned foundations nor institutes bears any responsibility for information contained in this publication. We also wish to thank the research assistance of James Kirkhope and research interns Adam Barrer, Melissa Brewster, John Evans, Kim Fadden, Meredith Gilchrist, Bryan Koontz, Jr., Alon Lanir, Vivek Narayanan, Manuel Pabon, Veris Prasarntree, Jay Rosen, Chris Rush, Rajarshi Sen, and Joseph Stephenson at the International Center for Terrorism Studies (Potomac Institute for Policy Studies) and Inter-University Center for Legal Studies (International Law Institute).

Yonah Alexander
and
Edgar H. Brenner
Washington, DC
June 8, 2001

About the Editors and Contributors

Professor Yonah Alexander is Senior Fellow and Director, International Center for Terrorism Studies, Potomac Institute for Policy Studies, as well as Director, Inter-University for Terrorism Studies and Co-Director, Inter-University Center for Legal Studies. He has published over 70 books in the field of terrorism and international affairs and is founding editor of *Terrorism: An International Journal*. He is co-editor with Prof. Edgar H. Brenner of a four-volume set on *Legal Aspects of Terrorism in the United States* (Oceana Publishers, 2000).

Professor Edgar H. Brenner is Co-Director of the Inter-University Center for Legal Studies in Washington, D.C.; he is also Legal Counsel to the Inter-University Center for Terrorism Studies. He has lectured on various aspects of counterterrorism policy at such venues as The George Washington University, Tel Aviv University, Marmara University Law School (Istanbul, Turkey), University of Michigan Law School and at Carleton College, Northfield, Minnesota. He is an advisor to the International Center for Terrorism Studies, Potomac Institute for Policy Studies.

Dr. Stephen P. Cohen is a Senior Fellow in the Foreign Policy Program of the Brookings Institution and is also an adjunct professor at Georgetown University. He retired as a professor of history and political science from the University of Illinois in 1998, where he continues to hold the title of Senior Research Scientist in the program in Arms Control, Disarmament and International Security.

Dr. M. Anthony Fainberg has a Ph.D. in high-energy physics from the University of California, Berkeley. He has served as Director of the Office of Policy and Planning for Aviation Security at the Federal Aviation Administration.

Dr. Christopher C. Joyner is Professor of Government at Georgetown University, where he teaches courses on international law and organizations, U.S. foreign policy, and global environmental law. He serves on the Executive Council of the American Society of International Law. He is a frequent consultant to various organizations, including the United States Senate and the Foreign Service Institute.

Martin Mendelsohn, Esq. is a partner in the law firm of Verner, Liipfert, Bernhard & Hand. His practice concentrates on trade and commercial issues between the United States and the emerging economies of post-Soviet Europe. He has served as a foreign policy advisor to senior members of the United States Senate and has been consulted by various foreign governments.

Michael J. O'Neil, Esq., for 22 years served as chief counsel for the House Intelligence Committee. He is a former General Counsel of the Central Intelligence Agency and is now in private law practice in Washington, D.C.

Dr. Wayne H. Zaideman has served as the Unit Chief for International Terrorism Analysis at the Federal Bureau of Investigation.

I.
Selected Topics

Terrorism: A Definitional Focus

Yonah Alexander

Many governments have failed to appreciate the extent and implications of the terrorist threat to modern societies. As a result, a large number of countries, including Western democracies, have not developed strong commitments to deal effectively with the challenge. A major reason for this failure is the definitional and moral confusion over what constitutes terrorism.[1] Every sovereign state reserves to itself the political and legal authority to define terrorism in the context of domestic and foreign affairs. And yet, some governments speak with a bewildering variety of voices on the subject of terrorism. The United States is a case in point.

In the U.S. federal system, each state determines what constitutes an offense under its criminal or penal code. States have therefore defined terrorism generically as a crime, thus ending the true need for the use of specific statutes covering other selected criminal acts that are identified as terrorism. For instance, the Arkansas Criminal Code states that "a person commits the offense of terroristic threatening if with the purpose of terrorizing another person, he threatens to cause death or serious physical injury or substantial property damage to another person."[2]

In general, state laws appear under nine separate headings, including civil defense (interstate compacts and state emergency management plans), antiterrorism provisions, destructive devices, terrorist threats, enhanced criminal penalties, victim compensation, street terrorism, ecological terrorism, and taxes.[3] Regarding the first category, as an example, the authority of states to enter into interstate compacts of any kind is governed by Article I, Section IV, Clause 3 of the United States Constitution, which requires congressional authorization. Similarly, the Disaster Relief and Emergency Assistance Act,[4]

---

[1] For sources on the definitional issues of terrorism as well as for literature on the general topic of terrorism, see, for instance, Yonah Alexander, ed., *Terrorism: An International Resource File*, 1986-1990 (Ann Arbor, Michigan: UMI, 1991).

[2] Ark. Code Ann. Section 5-13-301.

[3] The Ohio Code provides for tax abatements for certain victims of terrorism. Ohio Rev. Code Ann. 5747.023

[4] 42 USC 5195-5197f.

as amended, authorize interstate compacts dealing with civil defense against various emergencies, including terrorist incidents.[5]

In the legislative branch, it is also evident that no consensus has been reached. Indeed, over the past 30 years, the U.S. Congress has held numerous hearings, considered bills, adopted resolutions, and passed laws on terrorism.[6] Nevertheless, a comprehensive working definition that can address the different forms of terrorist attacks has not emerged from Congress thus far. Similarly, the executive branch, partly as a result of the very nature of its jurisdictional diversities, has not developed a coordinated position on the meaning of the term. Since the 1980s, for instance, the Federal Bureau of Investigation (FBI) has defined terrorism as "the unlawful use of force or violence against persons or property to intimidate or coerce a government, the civilian population, or any segment thereof, in the furtherance of political or social objectives." [7]

In recent years, however, the Department of State has adopted a definition, which is contained in Title 22 of the United States Code, Section 2656f(d), stating that "the term 'terrorism' means premeditated, politically motivated violence perpetrated against noncombatant targets by subnational groups or clandestine agents, usually intended to influence an audience." [8] Moreover, "the term 'international terrorism' means terrorism involving citizens of the territory of more than one country" [9] and "the term 'terrorist group' means any group practicing, or that has significant subgroups that practice international terrorism."[10]

Other countries, such as the United Kingdom, adopted an evolutionary definitional process of the meaning of what terrorism is. In 1996, for in-

---

[5]   For details, see Yonah Alexander and Edgar H. Brenner eds., *Legal Responses to Terrorism: U.S. State Legislation* (Dobbs Ferry, N.Y.: Oceana Publications, 2000).

[6.]   A recent oversight hearing on terrorist threats to the United States was held by the Subcommittee on Immigration and Claims, Committee on the Judiciary, U.S. House of Representatives, January 25, 2000, see News Advisory, January 24, 2000. For a bill initiated to establish a commission on aviation security and terrorism, seeking to investigate the destruction of Pan Am 103 on December 21, 1988 and KAL on August 31, 1983, see H.R. 2507 (101st Congress, 1st session, May 25, 1989).

[7.]   U.S. Department of Justice, FBI, *Terrorism in the United States, 1988.* (Terrorist Research and Analytical Center, Counterterrorism Section, Criminal Investigative Division, December 31, 1988), p. 34.

[8.]   22 USC § 2656f (d).

[9.]   *Id.*

[10.]   22 USC § 2656; Cited in Yonah Alexander and Donald Musch, *Terrorism: Documents of International and Local Control,* (Dobbs Ferry, N.Y.: Oceana Publications, 1999) Vol. 17, pp. 170-171.

stance, Lord Lloyd's inquiry into the future of antiterrorism legislation proposed, at the time, the following definition of terrorism: "the use of serious violence against persons or property, or the threat to use such violence, to intimidate or coerce a government, the public, or any section of the public, in order to promote political, social, or ideological objectives."[11] Under the 1999 Prevention of Terrorism Bill, the British government is proceeding with an even broader definition of terrorism that would include expressions of single-issue extremism by groups, such as the Animal Liberation Front. The latest definition of terrorism by the United Kingdom is as follows: "the use or threat, for purposes of advancing a political, religious, or ideological course of action which involves serious violence against any person or property, endangers the life of any person, or creates a serious risk to the health or safety of the public or a section of the public."[12]

Subsequently, the 1999 Prevention of Terrorism Bill completed its committee stages, proceeded to the House of Lords, and then became the Terrorism Act 2000. It went through a three-stage process. The major one being the the Terrorism Act 2000 (Commencement No 3) Order (SI 2000/421) which brought into force all the remaining provisions of the 2000 Act on 19 February 2001. The only provision not yet brought into force is s.100 providing for a code of practice on silent video recordings of interviews conducted by the Royal Ulster Constabulary or the Royal Ulster Constabulary Reserve.(A code had been made under s.53 of the Northern Ireland (Emergency Provisions) Act 1996, and is apparently being kept in place).

The definition of 'terrorism' is set out in s.1 of the Terrorism Act 2000. It is a two part definition. Section 1(1)provides that 'terrorism' means the use or threat of action where the action falls within subsection (2) (i.e. violence, serious damage, endangering life etc.)and "(b) the use or threat is designed to influence the government or to intimidate the public or a section of the public, and (c) the use or threat is made for the purpose of advancing a political, religious or ideological cause."

Section 1(1)(b) and (c) are therefore concerned with the purposes for which the action is taken or threatened. The substance of the relevant 'action' is defined in section 1(2, as follows;

"(2)Action falls within this subsection if it-

---

[11]   See, Lord Lloyd, "Inquiry into Legislation Against Terrorism," House of Lords, March 1996; and Yonah Alexander and Michael Noone, *Three Nations' Response to Terrorism* (The Hague: Martinus Nijhoff, 1997).

[12]   Quoted by Mark Matfield, "Terrorism Bill Passes Second Reading," in *RDS Newsletter* (January 2000), pp. 8-9. This quarterly also covers some of the latest activities of the Animal Liberation Front (ALF). For views of the ALF, see, for example, its Frontline Information Service: hhtp://www.enviroweb.org/ALFIS/index2.shtml

(a) involves serious violence against a person,

(b) involves serious damage to property,

(c) endangers a person's life, other than that of the person committing the action,

(d) creates a serious risk to the health or safety of the public or a section of the public, or

(e) is designed seriously to interfere with or disrupt and electronic system."

One should note an element of extra-territoriality in that 'action' is defined in s.1(4)(a) as including action outside the United Kingdom, and 'government' includes the government of a country outside the UK.

Section 1(2)(e) is no doubt designed to be up-to-date so as to cope with targeted hacking, but it could produce some odd results. If, for example, Greenpeace were to threaten to disrupt a government computer system (e.g. for dealing with oil revenues in Iraq) in order to put pressure on that Government over its treatment of the Kurds, it could be committing an act of terrorism for the purposes of the Terrorism Act. This example shows just how widely the concept of 'terrorism' is drawn.

Thus, definitional approaches of the United States and the United Kingdom reflect a divergence of national dispositions vis-à-vis terrorism. Similarly, international organizations, such as the United Nations, failed for decades to agree on a common universal definition. While both the United Nations General Assembly and the Security Council repeatedly affirmed their determination to combat terrorism in all its forms "irrespective of motive, wherever and by whomever committed,"[13] the world body was reluctant for political reasons to define precisely the nature of the terrorism challenge.

At any rate, the most detailed latest effort by the United Nations to craft a definition occurred in December 1999 when the General Assembly adopted by consensus the text of a draft International Convention for the Suppression of the Financing of Terrorism. It states that terrorism is

> "Criminal acts intended or calculated to
> provoke a state of terror in the general
> public, a group of persons or particular
> persons for political purposes are in any
> circumstances unjustifiable, whatever the
> considerations of a political, philosophical,
> ideological, racial, ethnic, religious, or

[13] UN Security Council Resolution 1269 (1999) at its 4053rd meeting, 19 October 1999.

other nature, that may be invoked to justify them." [14]

In short, an analysis of various governmental and intergovernmental, as well as academic views on the subject indicates that there is no consensus of what terrorism is.[15] Nevertheless, there seems to be an agreement related to its several components, such as the nature of the act (e.g., unlawful); perpetrators (e.g., individuals, groups, states); objectives (e.g., political); intended outcomes and motivations (e.g., fear and frustration); targets (e.g., victims); and methods (e.g., hostage taking).[16]

On the basis of these elements, is it reasonable to adopt the following working definition: terrorism is defined as the calculated employment or the threat of violence by individuals, subnational groups, and state actors to attain political, social, and economic objectives in the violation of law, intended to create an overwhelming fear in a target area greater than the victims attacked or threatened.

[14.] UN General Assembly Resolution 54/109, 9 December 1999.

[15.] See, for example, Alex P. Schmid and Albert J. Jongman, *Political Terrorism* (Amsterdam: North Holland Publishing Co., 1988), pp. 1-39.

[16.] Ray S. Cline and Yonah Alexander developed these elements in an unclassified report prepared for the U.S. Army on *State Sponsored Terrorism* (1985), pp. 22-23.

Terrorism and Genocide

Dr. Stephen P. Cohen

The twentieth century was the most violent century in the history of mankind. The estimates are that 110 to 120 million people have been violently killed. This took place through a mixture of war, genocide, and so-called natural disaster. Most of the natural disasters of this century have actually been man-made disasters, famines, floods, or some other human act, not necessarily by "nature."

The most prominent murderers of our era have been a very small number of people—Hitler, Stalin, Mao, Pol Pot, and a few others. Hopefully, we'll get through the century without new names added to the list.

War, genocide, and famine, or natural famine in particular, are often interlinked and associated. They often occur at the same time and in the same place. In fact, famines are used as an instrument of genocide, and genocide is often a by-product of war. Wars can trigger the kinds of passions (or incentives) that lead to genocides. There is no clear relationship between them except that they are cross-linked.

I don't think that there is necessarily a causal relationship between terrorism and either war, genocide, or famine. Terrorism is both an ends and a means, an instrument of policy, usually conducted by a small group, to pursue its objectives and its means. Simply put, terrorism is a function of political pathology. Terrorism arises because of the inability or the incompetence or political systems to cope with pathological groups in their societies, or to deal with fundamental problems of governance.

I don't think there's necessarily a relationship between terrorism and genocide, but increasingly, they occur at the same time. Until very recently, genocide was not considered a crime. It was perfectly legitimate to slaughter as many people as you could find if they were of a suitable ethnic, ideological, or other persuasion. There are four or five kinds of genocide that the literature has identified. I won't go through them all, but they include "conquest genocide," in which one group destroys another or displaces it. "Retributive genocide" takes place where there is rivalry between societies or between groups. Third, "political genocides" usually occur after a struggle for power. We've seen this in Rwanda. The classic example is that of the Athenian destruction of the Melians, described by Thucydides, in which the Athenians simply wiped out the people of Melos for daring to resist. It sounds as if it was written yesterday. And finally there's a contemporary invention, a variant on form of genocide, "ideological genocide," that is often accompanied by famine and war, and is done for a particular political purpose.

The modern contribution to genocide has been the development of a so-called scientific justification of genocide. In the past, people killed each other because they wanted to or they needed the space. It was you or us, ordinary "human" reasons. Today, genocides are often carried out in terms of a higher cause: Leninism, Stalinism, Nazism, or something else. You identify a particular group, and define them in such a way that their existence is scientifically proven to be repugnant, and then you eliminate them.

What we've seen in the past few years is simply a recurrence of traditional forms of genocide, old-fashioned genocides of one sort or another. I don't think we're likely to see the reoccurrence of the new form of genocide based on ideology or doctrine, I certainly hope not. That happens to be the most dangerous and the most inflammatory, causing the greatest number of deaths.

As for the role, or rule, of law, I've always seen this as a deep contradiction. Societies, whether state societies or international societies, come together and they create laws in order to force people to settle disputes by peaceful means. To do that, they themselves must use force. I think this is the essential dilemma of all politics. To have a just society, to have a society governed by law, you must in fact use force. The chances are five times out of 10 perhaps that the application of that force will be unjust, thereby creating new resentments and hatreds, which then lead to terrorism and other forms of political pathologies. So I think that human beings are essentially stuck with a dilemma. The more human beings there are, the more we'll see this occur around the world. I don't foresee any diminution of conflicts between states or within states. On the other hand, I don't foresee the rise of new ideological forms of genocide, which, in this century, were the most destructive of all.

Martin Mendelsohn, Esq.

I'm going to expand a bit on what Professor Cohen mentioned and that is the rule of law and its application in the prevention of terrorism and the prevention of genocide. The problem, of course, is that the rule of law has failed in this regard. This century is one of bloody conflict. We coined the term "The Great War" for the First World War. After the First World War, the victorious allies insisted that there be war crimes trials and they were held in Germany. They were judged a failure as most of the sentences were either nonexistent or light and the effort was soon abandoned. By 1921, everything was a "return to normalcy." And, of course, we then had the Kellogg-Briand Pact of 1928, which outlawed war. And I need not tell you that by the middle of the 1930s, war was raging in Asia, and by the end of the 1930s, in Europe, despite the pact and despite everything else.

The United States was drawn into the war at the end of 1941, and once again we attempted to impose a system of values and law in the resolution of war crimes and the conflict. The allies met in Moscow in 1943, and issued the declaration that there would be trials for war crimes at the end of the war. They set up a procedure. Most of the allies signed immediately. Virtually, all of the puppet states, then puppets to the Soviet Union, signed as well, and the Nuremberg process began in 1945.

First, with the International Military Tribunal, which tried the high-level Nazis and then smaller tribunals, which, if my memory serves, existed until about 1951 when lesser individuals were tried at the same time. The occupying force, basically the United States Army, conducted denazification hearings, and we tried to purify German society and create a democracy. I think we succeeded in creating a democracy, and we failed in purifying the society, whatever that might mean. In 1951, the U.S. High Commissioner for Germany essentially gutted the process, commuted most of the sentences, and everyone was returned to society; and there we sat in 1951.

There is not a direct causation, however, between what happened in 1951 and subsequent events in the world. The terrible lessons of history are that when genocide or attempted extermination of the people occurs, it only seems to attract our attention if it's in Europe. We can talk about what happened to the Jews and earlier to the Ukrainians by Stalin, where famine was used as a weapon, and perhaps as many as 20 million people died and this is in the 1930s, before hostilities began. But, if it occurs in Cambodia or in the continent of Africa, we seem not to know about it or care about it or do anything about it. And that's one of the tragedies.

My personal belief is, as awful and terrible and reprehensible as the actions of the Milosevic government may be, it does not amount to genocide, and we have probably overreacted or underreacted, depending upon one's view in trying to deal with this. The only thing I can convince others is what we're doing is not quite the right thing, certainly not within the rule of law. The Yugoslavs, as you may know, have brought suit in the World Court against ten of the North Atlantic Treaty Organization countries asking for the World Court to rule on whether the action is legal within the UN Charter or within the customary norms of international law.

The problems that we have in attempting to call for the imposition of the rule of law in these activities is that we have no enforcement mechanism. Terrorism can easily degenerate or graduate, depending upon one's view, into genocide, and we are faced with the necessity of seeking political solutions to problems that may not be subject to political solutions because of the element of force that's involved. I don't want to sound overly pessimistic because I've been involved in a number of cases that have used American courts to seek justice against those malefactors, and we've been moderately successful. However, it remains an issue as between governments whether governments can do anything to properly enforce the Rule of Law and impose sanctions for those nations that are deemed to be outside the family of nations.

Prof. Christopher C. Joyner

I think in a real sense genocide personifies the horrors of mass terrorism perpetrated by governments and paramilitary groups against their own citizens, as well as against their own neighbors. Professor Cherif Bassiouni of De Paul University has referred to this as tyrannical regime victimization, which sounds very "social sciencey", but I think it provides a real important insight into the horrors of the twentieth century. Rudy Rummel, in a book called *Death by Government* in 1994, put the estimate of persons killed by their own governments at 170 million in this century.

What I find most distinctly disturbing about these tragedies is that there have been so few prosecutions of the perpetrators of these mass killings. In fact, since the Nuremberg trials and the Tokyo war crimes trials, there have been tens of millions of people also killed in genocidal atrocities, but there have only been two internationally created ad hoc tribunals to prosecute perpetrators. There have only been two investigatory commissions. Both those, of course, were for the former Yugoslavia and Rwanda. There has been only one international truth commission for El Salvador. There have been only two national prosecutions of other nationals, namely those involving Ethiopia and Rwanda. There have been some select national prosecutions in Chile and Argentina. And there has been a special body created in South Africa called the Truth and Reconciliation Commission. There have also been some so-called lustration laws used in East and Central European countries, but few of those have imposed prosecution on the perpetrators. Most of those people have been prohibited from participating in political office.

What I'm suggesting to you in this era of terrorism and genocide is that the victims are many, but those who are brought to justice are few. The question that I think important is to appreciate why. Why have so few perpetrators been brought to justice? I think the answer is that all too frequently; justice is bartered away for political settlement. That, in fact, impunity is the price we pay for a cessation of violence in many of these civil conflicts, especially in the developing world. And you use impunity as a way of providing the grease for lubricating the transition from one tyrannical regime to a regime change.

And so what I'm suggesting to you is that justice becomes the victim all too often of realpolitik. The grim reality as we see in the case of Milosevic is that if there's going to be a peace settlement arrived at, you negotiate with the butcher and that, unfortunately, gives rise to the offer of impunity down the road.

Truth commissions have been suggested as an interim measure between doing nothing and formal prosecution. South Africa was a very bold experiment along those lines. I personally have problems with the South African Truth and Reconciliation Commission because I don't think the purging of truth can serve as a substitute for justice. I don't think confessing one's sins and admitting that you bashed a man's head against a prison cell wall and killed him is sufficient to allow for your going free, to avoid being tried and prosecuted for that crime.

One of the lessons of impunity from genocide that we've learned over the past fifty years is that if there is going to be the rule of law, then there's going to have to be greater consideration given for reversing this trend towards impunity. And that means there are certain rights that have to be upheld in the course of the post-conflict restoration of civil order in these societies. One of these rights that has to be ensured is the victim's right to know. The victim's right to know who did this to him or her, and why. There is also, I think, a need for the state -- indeed, a duty of the state — to remember the gross violations of human rights that result in genocide so that in the future, this memory can serve as a possible deterrent against these crimes happening again. I think there is also a fundamental right of the victim's right to justice. No just and lasting reconciliation in a society can occur, in my view, unless there is an effective response for justice, and impunity, of course, undermines that response.

Let me set forth a number of don'ts that I think are very important, don'ts which I think would reverse this trend towards impunity, but obviously which depend upon the political will of governments to enforce. And if governments are not willing to make these things happen, then impunity will persist as the trend in responding to genocide.

I think it's important, as a don't, not to grant freedom or amnesty to perpetrators of gross violations of human rights unless victims have been ensured some other course of redress. I think there is a very important "don't" in granting the right of asylum to any perpetrator of genocide, crimes against humanity, war crimes, or torture. States should not lawfully give asylum to those kinds of offenders. I think there's a very important don't in terms of providing safe haven under the guise of the political offense exception from extradition, or to put it to you in a positive sense, if there is a perpetrator of genocide—an offender of genocide who has been apprehended in one state—there is a legal obligation to extradite or prosecute that offender. Do not give that person safe haven.

By the same token, I think there is an important "don't" in permitting some individual in the armed forces to have an offense ameliorated on grounds of defense of superior orders. International law says—and since Nuremberg, this has been the rule—if you are ordered to commit an international crime such as genocide, a war crime, or a crime against humanity, that will not serve as an excuse to mitigate your offense. I think that's a very important rule to keep intact.

And also certainly true, I think it's a very important don't that military courts be used to try perpetrators of human rights violations that are perpetrated against civilians. I think military courts should be limited to prosecuting military persons for military offenses. Let the civilian courts try the human rights violators. All too often, those who commit the crimes are military personnel.

In the final analysis, as we all know, international law is not automatic. International law is not self-enforcing. If there is going to be a reversal of this awful trend in the line of impunity, it will have to come from the governments themselves. And the United States, I think, must take a lead in that role. I think genocide, in general, and terrorism in particular, are going to really remain very much with us during this coming century unless the members of the Security Council of the United Nations and the United States in particular take a leading role in trying to reverse that trend.

Aviation Security: Case Study

Dr. M. Anthony Fainberg

I will speak on the perspective of aviation security, both domestic and overseas, to give you a quick view and to remind you of major events within the last ten years. The perspective begins with a long series of acts against aviation over the 1980s but for the United States, the culmination was Pan Am 103. Even though it took place overseas, it was an act directed at an American aircraft leaving the United Kingdom and destined for New York City. That event triggered a large change in the way people in the United States considered the issue of aviation security. Until that point, there had been very strong resistance by air carriers, in particular, to instituting procedures and placing technologies to prevent the introduction of explosive devices and other dangerous items aboard aircraft. The interesting thing is that the technologies that were able to detect explosives (in the quantities that were sufficient to bring down aircraft) were just at the point of being developed, but were not quite yet there. So we relied on requiring a number of procedures both domestically and overseas for flights into the United States. One of the things that we did require, in fact, was that a passenger be matched to a bag; in other words, that a bag should not be placed aboard an aircraft unless there was a passenger with it. We did have regulations to that effect, but they were not followed from Frankfurt where, the result was, as you know, that a bag with a bomb in it, apparently, was introduced from a flight from Malta and transferred in Frankfurt to the Pan Am aircraft. The flight flew over to London. Then, en route from London to New York, it detonated. The procedures were down and in place but they were not implemented. And I would say that they were not implemented in great part because the air carrier in question did not take the threat as seriously as they should have; they were concerned more about saving money than they were at seriously looking at the requirements. As a result of that, there was a large explosion, of course, in Congress, as well as above Scotland. And there were several pressure groups created by the relatives of the people who died. These pressure groups have been extremely successful in raising interest, and the efforts have resulted in the promulgation of laws and regulations regarding aviation security. A very useful history in that respect: the disaster gave rise to a group of public interest people that actually changed things.

What is kind of interesting is that Pan Am 103 really set the trigger for implementing effective aviation security measures. What happened then was that a lot of money went into research to develop the technologies that were on the verge, but were not quite there—technologies that were able to detect bombs in suitcases that would be placed aboard an aircraft. And structural changes were made within the Federal Aviation Administration, raising the importance and the profile of aviation security within the body. And for those of you who know about government organizations: even though you may have something within the Federal Aviation Administration called security, it's very important to know exactly where that security organization fits within the structure to understand how influential it will or will not be.

Before 103, security constituted a very small organization with very little power and influence. After 103, it became one of what are the seven principal lines of business within the Federal Aviation Administration with an associate administrator who is my boss: one of seven equals within the agency. Then, people took security much more seriously from an organizational perspective.

There were many other things that were required by Congress in the Aviation Security Improvement Act of 1990 that we had to do, including ways in which we put agents out in the field, to whom they reported, and an oversight body external to the agency over our Research and Development.

An interesting result was that some years later, in 1996, we had TWA 800, which ironically turned out not to have been a terrorist action. At that point things were in place for some real action to be accomplished. Now, all the time between 1990 and 1996, the Federal Aviation Administration developed useful technologies, and we had a larger number of people in the field, both domestically and internationally, to monitor aviation security. But in terms of putting the technologies that were really effective out there in the airports, we still got a push back from the air carriers who, (a), said there were no serious threats, and (b), did not want to be burdened with the cost of the technologies and the additional cost in training quality people to work security.

What was ironic is that TWA 800, as I said, was almost certainly not a terrorist act. The trigger that had been set—the governmental trigger that had been set by one of the results of Pan Am 103 - was finally let go. You had a presidential commission run by the vice president of the country making sweeping decisions on changes in aviation security. This forced a complete (not to coin a phrase) "paradigm shift" in the way the country regarded aviation security. Not only the Congress, but the air carriers and the airports changed their perspectives. As a result, there were some decisions that were made that were rather important—one of which was that 100 million dollars per year was allocated by Congress (now for three years)—to purchase explosives detection and other security equipment and get it out there. This circumvented, to a degree, the issue of the air carriers that they didn't want to spend the money to purchase rather expensive equipment.

We have developed explosive detectors that are able to detect bombs in suitcases to the degree that is required and that do not have devastating impacts on the operations and the flow of passengers and bags aboard aircraft. This deployment is still underway, and it's only about, I would say, 25 percent complete now. We'll continue it over the next few years. What I'm talking about includes not just equipment for detecting bombs and checked baggage, but also equipment that will be detecting bombs and other dangerous objects at check points where carry on bags are inspected. Eventually, equipment will include things that are able to detect explosives on the person's bodies.

In 1994 and 1995, we had the additional shock of the Ramzi Yousef affair in the Philippines. This was a plan by a gentleman who is called Ramzi Yousef (although that's not his real name, that's what he's generally known as) who is currently in prison. He was involved in the World Trade Center business and then left the country, escaped the net that got most of his colleagues, went to southeast Asia, and was manufacturing explosives, bombs, and trying to put them on some 12 U.S. aircraft departing various locations in southeast Asia. He was planning to do that in early 1995, but he had a fire in his laboratory that was in his apartment in Manila at the end of 1994.

And eventually after a long series of pursuits and posted rewards for his capture, he was finally brought to justice in Pakistan, having been turned in by somebody who accepted their reward from the Department of State. He then was brought back here for trial for the World Trade Center affair. I give you all of this to tell you that this happened just before the TWA incident, kind of setting the immediate stage for the reaction to the crash and heightening people's interest in improving aviation agency security at that point.

TWA 800 resulted in the U.S. government and the air transport industry actually carrying things out. Mr. Yousef actually had put a very small bomb on a Philippine Airlines aircraft, from a provincial airport to Manila. He got off in Manila: the plane flew off to on to Japan. The bomb detonated and killed one person, but the aircraft was brought safely to the ground in Okinawa. That was apparently a test run in preparation for 12 other rather major runs that he was planning. From our perspective, the security perspective, the interest is that he didn't put the bomb in checked baggage as was done in Pan

Am 103. He carried it; he carried the bomb either in carry-on bags or in his pockets, and presumably this was the path that was going to be used for the 12 events that he was scheduling.

What we have done domestically is take the 100 million dollars a year allocated by Congress and spent about half of it on checked baggage security, spending the rest on carry-on and checkpoint security. Combine that with a whole series of changes, upgrades, and improvements that will improve the process of protecting the aircraft from illegitimate and dangerous devices.

The system we have now domestically, touching on some interest of legal aspects, is as follows: note this has been accomplished so far voluntarily with air carriers who, as I have said, have followed a paradigm shift towards being more proactive and, at least on the surface, being much more interested in doing something significant to prevent terrorism.

What we do first is use a computer system that takes the information that's in the reservation system (the passenger name record) and looks at it. The computer takes that information and excludes from consideration maybe 95 percent of the people about whom the system thinks we know enough so that we do not consider them a threat. The remaining people have their bags checked and submit to security checks or bag matching. This is the system that is now being implemented across the country.

The screening system raises civil liberties issues, because people will say, "Well, on what basis are you selecting the five percent of us for additional security measures?" Now, in the first place, the response is that additional security measures are not particularly burdensome. These do not involve nasty questions, a strip search, or being delayed. What they involve is that the bags will either be put through one of these x-ray viewing devices that we're purchasing or being matched to the individual. In other words, the bags won't be transported unless you get on the aircraft yourself.

But nevertheless, there have been some people in the community who have been objecting to this, on the grounds that we are unfairly selecting people of Middle Eastern origin, particularly Arabs or Arab Americans. The response to that is that we are not telling anybody exactly what it is that we use to make the selection of some or the nonselection of others. But these do not include ethnic, gender, race, religion, or any such characteristics. They merely include the mechanisms under which you engaged the purchase of your ticket. We have been allowed by the Department of Justice to have access to exactly how we select, and an independent review has approved the nondiscriminatory nature of the process. We're performing ongoing studies to assure that there is no bias towards people of any particular racial or religious group.

The regulatory process that we're undertaking involves making these security measures a requirement. Right now, it's entirely voluntary among the carriers and is being carried out actually quite successfully.

I've learned that being, among other things, in charge of our rule making process, that rules are not made in a day. In fact I've been kind of shocked by how long it takes some rules to be put into place. When I came on board, I discovered that there are some major security rules regarding screening procedures for screening that prevent the wrong people from having access to sensitive areas of airports. These rules were started in 1987 and 1988, and they're still not complete. The notice of proposed rule making for this set of upgrades to our security rules for airports and air carriers was published some two years ago and finally will come to fruition in a final ruling in about four or five months.

In general, rule making in the Federal Aviation Administration takes a long time for a number of reasons—one of which is, you have to have a lot of interaction with stakeholders before a rule can clear the Federal Aviation Administration. Another difficulty is that the Federal Aviation Administration is part of the Department of Transportation. So when we clear a rule from Federal Aviation Administration and this takes quite awhile, it then goes over to the office of the Secretary of Transportation, where it also stays a significant amount of time. From our perspective, this provides a great deal of difficulty because if there are serious security issues, it may take a long time before you could get your rule through. And when you get the rule through, objective situations that required a rule may have changed substantially; this is one of the issues we have deal with. Eventually, a rule has to pass through the Office of Management and Budget, too, because you have to understand how much the rule is costing the country in relation to how much it benefits the country. You also have to make sure you don't adversely impact small businesses.

On one occasion we actually produced a rule in 24 hours. Now, that was when we discovered—because of a TV news program around Thanksgiving two and a half years ago—that people were getting access to airports in the guise of security screeners or ramp operators by presenting false information. The right procedures weren't being performed to check on this. We found out that actually, in 24 hours, you could put through a rule you considered an emergency. And the emergency was that the American public (or about 100 million people) learned about the matter on TV, some 24 hours earlier.

So there are good things you can do with rule making, but these are generally matters of extreme urgency. The question of bag-match or screening of baggage through our high technology equipment is something we were told was a high priority of the vice president in December of 1997. We were excoriated because we couldn't put the rule out in two months; we gave it to them in three months. But because of the cumbersome process, the notice of the rulemaking was published here just recently.

I haven't touched upon the international aspects of counter-terrorism as it relates to aviation security. There, a lot of the leverage you have comes from the International Civil Aviation Organization, which published recommended security measures. Voluntary measures are supposed to be applied by all countries to prevent unwanted things from happening: for example, bags not accompanying people internationally. These measures have been in place for a number of years. They are not being applied—everywhere, but more and more countries are signing up to them, particularly our partners in Europe. We also have bilateral agreements with many foreign countries regarding aviation security. Bilateral agreements are with those countries from whom you can fly directly into the United States. These are touchy issues and have to do with sovereignty and a large range of other international issues.

We require a certain level of security on aircraft coming into the United States directly from many cities overseas. Some of these cities are considered to be relatively high risk because of past terrorist activities in those areas. So we exert leverage over other foreign countries saying, you must apply such and such security measures to our carriers leaving your land and coming to our country. If you don't want to do that, we won't let any of your airplanes land in this country. This is the ultimate leverage which is generally, not spoken but which is used implicitly.

There is a current rule-making going on now in which we actually require identical security measures for U.S. and foreign carriers coming into and leaving this country. Foreign countries consider this interference in their sovereignty and consider that we're doing only for economic reasons to level the economic playing field. They argue that U.S. air carriers are much more serious targets and require higher security measures in general. There are exceptions, like Sri Lanka and Israel, but, in general, U.S. air carriers are higher profile targets. Other countries say: "Well, if you want to protect your carriers at a higher level, that makes sense because the threat is higher. But don't make us spend money on this, since our threat is lower." We are involved in a rule-making process to require identical measures. This has very interesting international implications, and I don't know how the matter is going to be resolved.

Well, I've gone through a number of legal and quasi-legal issues, trying to give you general idea of what's going on in civil aviation security in this country, and to a degree in the world. We are in a transition period ranging up from virtually no effective technology to some very effective technology. This ramp up could take another few years. The good thing about it is that our adversaries don't know exactly where all our equipment is and how good it is. If nothing else, it functions as a deterrent at least in the short term. In the longer term we had better make sure the equipment gets out there and it all works. We are doing this.

Cyber-Terrorism: Case Study

Michael J. O'Neil, Esq.

The topic is combating cyber terrorism and information warfare. I will limit myself to asking how this very important goal can be squared with the protection of civil liberties and with the viability of commercial enterprises.

As I said, addressing this topic here in Washington, D.C. has become a familiar activity. The good news is that a speaker can count on an audience like this to understand the importance of certain key industries, key business sectors, to traditional national security needs, like troop mobilization, but also to agree that the normal operation of certain sectors—transportation, energy, power generation, water supply, finance, communications, emergency services, and essential government functions—are critical to our economic security as well. The bad news is that audiences outside the Capitol are much less likely to be paying attention to these matters.

Our imaginations do not have any trouble comprehending the need for infrastructure protection and the potentially terrible damage that a successful attack could accomplish. By now, the well-known example of the Solar Sunrise case provides a chilling reminder to all of us of how our unclassified defense systems can come under attack. We need only look at Tom Clancy and other writers of popular fiction to take us through scenarios in which key elements of our economy are also placed in danger.

There is much about the government's approach to this threat that deserves praise. It has identified the problem. It has proposed a sensible solution in the macro sense - that of a government-industry partnership. It has begun to plan and to organize, and it has committed funds, which is always important in this city. In short, it wants to help, and it admits that it doesn't have all of the answers.

With at least one striking exception, all of this is largely being ignored in corporate boardrooms, and the administration's efforts at educating businesses have been limited and low key. Critical infrastructure simply has not caught on, perhaps because of businesses' single-minded attention to the Y2K issue, most likely because there has not been a really big catastrophe to focus their minds and their pocketbooks on the problem.

Students of this latter phenomenon, a catastrophic terrorist attack, advance the idea that such an attack will be required to produce real change; and they suggest that a future disaster will so horrify us as a nation that we will immediately mobilize policy responses to the problem. This action will be taken swiftly, and they say at the expense of civil liberties. Such results are to be deplored, but they have to be anticipated.

I think that is an excellent point. It is one with which I strongly agree, and it is made all the more plausible by the nature of the Administration's approach to infrastructure protection.

First of all, the Administration has defined this issue as a national security problem, which as we all know typically involves the military and our security agencies.

Second, unlike other national security issues, the President is proposing an unusual partnership between government and the private sector, one which is cooperative, fully voluntary, centers on the sharing of information, and implemented not by national security directives, but by employing market, fiduciary, and public opinion pressures to produce improved cyber security.

So, if the information structures to make all of this work—computer defense centers is what Dick Clarke [National Security Council] likes to call them—are not in place or if related legislation which is now being considered has not been enacted, then there will be a rush to fix this problem. In the process, we may lose something, perhaps some civil liberties, certainly some clarity as to what it is we are agreeing to, and almost certainly the time to consider carefully what will be important choices for individual citizens as well as for the nation.

What are some of these unmade choices, and why are they best decided in calm deliberation? Let's take security standards, which have to be at the heart of this issue.

All of us would accept that computer security for key infrastructures should be strong enough to defeat any attack that would either disable them or deny operator control.

Who is to set these standards? The government says that it will help to do so, but it does not want to set them for systems that it does not own, control, and understand. It is, in fact, still working hard to protect its own nonclassified, but critical, systems; and it says that the metrics simply are not there yet for either those systems or for the private sector.

I would submit that it is strongly in the interest of business to hold government to that position. What any business wants to be able to do is to manage its own strategic planning, particularly decisions surrounding the assumption, timing, and cost of new security obligations. If, instead, new and unfamiliar standards are imposed suddenly from the outside, that obviously plays the devil with profit margins.

That is not an argument against better security, but it is one for better planning. Planning obviously involves figuring out what to do first. That, too, is best left to computer-system operators who understand their own systems better than anyone else.

In this interconnected world, every business needs secure information technology and cannot get it all in-house, but it and similar businesses often know better than outsiders how to apply such knowledge.

To repeat, the government does not disagree with this proposition, but if immediately after a catastrophic event that threatens, even if it never succeeds, to take down a major transportation hub, a financial center, or power grid, and if that event is the work of a terrorist or we think that it is, and if finally the Congress and the public discovers we have nothing in place to protect such systems, will we wait for these businesses to do voluntarily what many of us will then say they should have already done? I doubt that.

With the possibility of mandatory cyber security enhancements will come other "necessary improvements" because the instinct of those familiar with infrastructure protection concerns will be to provide, as experts in this audience would no doubt suggest, as comprehensive a solution as possible. So we will mandate improvements not just in computer security, but also in businesses' personnel security. While insisting that certain information be reported to the government, we will also seek to protect the proprietary business information in such reports from access to the public or to competitors. Of course, we will consider very seriously the need to arm law enforcement and intelligence agencies with the tools to pursue terrorists, criminals, spies, or malevolent hackers that we will by then fear more than we ever have in the past.

There is another area where uncommon speed may not serve the nation well over time. Most Americans strongly resist the idea that the government needs greater authority to monitor their communications or the Internet, and the Federal Bureau of Investigation has disavowed any plans to seek any greater monitoring authority for infrastructure protection than it can now employ under existing statutes. The Bureau has stressed that it can perform all its current and projected National Infrastructure Protection Center (NIPC) operations under current law, but that is not an opinion which is shared government wide, as was shown recently by the leak of a national plan for information systems protection and of something called the Federal Intrusion Detection Network (FIDNET).

FIDNET was to be a netted intrusion-detection monitoring system for non-Department of Defense government computers. It was modeled on an existing DOD system. Intrusion-detection monitors installed on individual systems or networks were to be netted, so that an intruder or an intrusion technique used at one site would be automatically known at all sites.

The FBI was to be at the center of the system, and raw or filtered data from the network of censors would have been provided to the NIPC at the FBI. Ultimately, the plan stated it was the goal to have similar monitoring censors installed on private-sector information systems, as well.

The plan clearly recognized that there were civil liberties implications to FIDNET: and it said, and I quote, "As access to relevant networks is premised on consent of the user to allow session monitoring, the collection of certain data identified as anomalous activity or a suspicious event would not be considered a privacy issue."

Legally, that is quite true. The Electronic Communications Privacy Act permits the owner of a computer system to monitor the use of its system in order to protect that system and its own equities therein.

FIDNET was immediately criticized as an ill-defined monitoring system of potentially broad sweep. Critics said that it placed monitoring and surveillance at the center of the government's response to the problem, something which it had earlier disavowed and which it continues to disavow.

Since then, the administration has completely redesigned FIDNET. It is now to be located at the General Services Administration (GSA), and their new description is as follows:

Attacking intrusion information would be gathered and analyzed by agency experts. Only data on system anomalies would be forwarded to GSA for further analysis. Law enforcement would receive information about computer attacks and intrusions only under longstanding legal rules where an agency determines there is sufficient indication of illegal conduct. The private sector is not linked in any automated or other new way to GSA under this program.

This does not indicate that the debate about FIDNET is over. Those within the Administration who favored the development of a widespread centralized system of monitoring for government and private-sector communication systems will continue to push their vision, and this is a perfect example of why there is need for continued oversight within the executive branch, the Congress, and the public.

 Moreover, the debate on FIDNET and the accompanying debate on encryption policy have highlighted the need for a broader look at legal standards governing the monitoring of communications.

In its most recent statement on FIDNET, the administration emphasized that it will be fully consistent with privacy law and practice. Current legal standards, however, offer little reassurance, for the Electronic Communication Privacy Act gives service providers a wide latitude in monitoring and intercepting communications on their own systems to protect their rights or their property.

Now, in the case of all critical infrastructures, moves to increase personnel security also raise serious privacy concerns. The Employee Polygraph Protection Act was adopted to address documented limitations on the polygraph and a long record of commercial abuses. The Presidential Commission on Critical Infrastructure Protection, which kicked off the issue of infrastructure protection, recommended weakening the Act's protections. Similarly, there was in the Commission's report a general suggestion of dissatisfaction with the rules on access to and use of criminal history records and other personally identifiable information, rules which have been forged over time and refined to provide protections against the misuse of records that are frequently incomplete, inaccurate, and otherwise unreliable.

Secrecy and classification are still other concerns. The Freedom of Information Act (FOIA) is a vital component of our system of openness and government accountability. Over the past decade, tremendous effort has been devoted to decreasing the amount of unnecessarily classified information. In many respects, the strength, the economic vitality, and the innovation in our new communications technologies are supported, not hindered, by openness. Therefore, amendments to the FOIA or increased use of national security information classification would raise concerns, especially because of the risk that statutory changes would be subjected to over-broad interpretation.

At the same time, corporations have a right to protect their proprietary information, information which the government is asking them to share in the common good. I believe that corporate information can be protected without increased use of the classification stamp or FOIA amendments. I think it is noteworthy that the FBI has concluded that existing FOIA law generally suffices to protect confidential private-sector information submitted to the NIPC as part of its infrastructure protection work. This places a heavy burden on any federal agency that would propose a change in the law.

The FBI has also said that it seeks no expansion of classification authorities. Nonetheless, the possible use of existing authority needs to be clarified by the FBI and by other federal agencies.

These are just some of the privacy concerns and the dangers of government regulation which serious infrastructure policy ought to address. In seeking to protect key national computer systems, we must spend equal energy and concern in avoiding the creation of serious impediments to industry, in protecting individual liberty, and in securing public acceptance of the government's proposals.

With this last and equally important goal in mind, I would propose a number of do's and don't's to be incorporated clearly in the government's official descriptions of an infrastructure protection plan and to be kept particularly in mind as we deal with the privacy issues that are raised by this problem.

First, there should be no government compulsion of information-sharing by the private sector. The voluntary nature of industry participation in infrastructure protection schemes is vital to the credibility of the government's approach. The private sector built and operates these infrastructures. It understands them best, and it must lead any effort to improve its security.

Second, there should be no mandated security fixes imposed by the government. There are already strong market forces to encourage good security practices, and industry already leads in such developments. Unless government also proposes to subsidize corporate budgets, this type of planning must be left to those who must also run the systems to be protected.

Third, the government has never run critical infrastructures and should not try to begin to do so. Thus, the government's protection role does not include directing protective or preventive measures, but encouraging and advising when it has unique knowledge or expertise.

Fourth, there is no need and no legal mechanism for government monitoring of private-sector information networks to protect critical infrastructures. Any such proposal to do so would offend both constitutional and legal guarantees of privacy and individual rights. I would add that if intrusion protection is the goal, this is a function that must be controlled by infrastructure owners and operators.

Fifth, no case has been made for the widespread use of polygraph tests for personnel involved in the operation of critical infrastructure companies. The use of this device for personnel security checks is already regulated by federal and state laws.

Sixth, there is no need for the imposition of national security classification controls and government personnel security rules in private-sector companies operating critical infrastructures. Systematic use of classification does not easily lend itself to private sector commerce and would add unnecessary cost and reduce efficiency, particularly in crises.

The FBI, which again has thought about this issue, will be the repository of sensitive business information acquired by the federal government for infrastructure protection, and it sees no need for amendments to the FOIA.

Now, those are the don't's. I think there ought to be at least two do's, which are, if anything, more important still.

First, government, academia, the private community, and industry associations have got to do everything possible to wake up corporate America and convince them to take critical infrastructure protection seriously.

Second, and most importantly, public congressional hearings should be held by the committees with jurisdiction on any proposals for statutory changes that may emerge, especially in the area of federal criminal law. Unfortunately, recent significant changes to, among other things, the federal wiretapping laws regarding roving wiretaps were accomplished by evading this process and the public debate that it fosters. This cannot become the pattern for consideration of such very important security and privacy issues which, more than anything else, need to be subjected to public scrutiny, debate, and refinement, and need to be subjected to that scrutiny sooner rather than later.

National Responses:
The Role of the Federal Bureau of Investigation
(Legal Attaché)

Dr. Wayne H. Zaideman

What is the role of the Legal Attaché overseas? The legal attaché (LEGAT) is the FBI Director's personal representative in the foreign countries where he/she resides and/or has regional responsibilities. The legal attachés strive for meaningful cooperation with the host governments around the world ... cooperation with these governments is now indispensable in countering the global terrorism threats. Good faith and trust are developed and nourished through these liaison contacts, and close working relationships are established between the legal Attaché and his host country counterparts. This enhances the ability of the FBI to maintain a proactive rather than merely a reactive posture regarding terrorist threats.

There has been expansion of the LEGAT program. Within the last several years this program has expanded dramatically. This is in response to the increased challenges posed by international terrorism and international crime. The FBI has seen the need to foster cooperation between various U.S. government agencies in the battle against international terrorism; but in addition, it is necessary to reach out to other countries and cultivate avenues of cooperation. We liaison with police and other services in the host countries in order to share information and request assistance on cases of common interest.

Although we establish offices overseas, we understand our limitations and perform our jobs while respecting the sovereignty of the host countries. The badge that I have carried for over twenty-one years while working in the United States does not have the same significance overseas. LEGAT cannot unilaterally interview individuals, collect evidence, and make arrests.

Requests for assistance are accomplished through close cooperation and trust. However, any request for evidence to be used in a legal proceeding is obtained through established consular channels. When we are requesting such material, it is done through formal requests for legal assistance known as "letters rogatory," and often within the provisions of a Mutual Legal Assistance Treaty (MLAT). [17]

Extradition is requested of criminals from one country to be turned over to the requesting country. The U.S. Department of Justice will set out the statutory basis, the facts in the case, and state promises of reciprocity. This request is transmitted by the U.S. Department of State to the Ministry of Justice in the host country through normal diplomatic channels. It should be noted that LEGAT cannot make arrests in foreign countries; they rely upon the host government for the arrest and detention of the subject.

Problems may arise. The subject's actions, which constituted a crime in the United States may not be a criminal act in his home country (e.g., money laundering). Also, his crime may be judged to be political, qualifying the subject for asylum. In some cases, the host country may have a law against extradition of its own citizens. In such cases, it may be necessary for the United States to conduct its prosecution in the host country, and the sentence will be served in the host country.

The LEGAT program is very important in maintaining operational connections and in conducting international training. By conducting international training with the host countries, we not only establish effective liaison, but also teach effective principles of law enforcement and counter-terrorism. This works toward effective institution building, sensitivity to human rights concerns, and the establishment of the rule of law in various countries.

In response to new challenges posed by international terrorism, the FBI created joint terrorism task forces both at the field office level and at the headquarters level. There has been a closing of distances we previously had in the past between the various U.S. government agencies. The need to work together on terrorism issues rather than each of us going in our own direction is evident.

In addition, three years ago the FBI formed the unit in which I am currently unit chief (the International Terrorism Analysis Unit) where we have a well-trained cadre of professional analysts that work on tactical analysis in support of ongoing investigations; and moving toward a greater emphasis on strategic analysis.

All of the above—the expanded legal attaché program, joint terrorism task forces, international terrorism training, and improved analysis—are all positive responses to the evolution of terrorist threats directed against the United States.

---

[17] Editors' Note: "letters rogatory" = formal communication in writing to a foreign country court or judge requesting that testimony of a witness resident may be taken under its direction and transmitted to the first court for use in a pending trial.

When we consider investigations on the use of the Internet by terrorists and terrorist groups, the FBI is sensitive to the attorney general guidelines and First Amendment issues. We must do our job to safeguard individuals within our country, while being sensitive to civil rights and liberties. One use of the Internet is to raise money for terrorist organizations by use of "front organizations"; another is to spread propaganda and to recruit. While some funds are used for "philanthropic" purposes, some are also used to buy bullets and bombs. It is often extremely difficult to trace which funds go for which purposes. Fundraising and material support for terrorist organizations are a criminal enterprise. Each year the Department of State sets out a list of organizations deemed to be terrorist organizations. This is sometimes referred to as the "dirty thirty list."

Intergovernmental Responses:
International Organizations and Law

Amb. (Ret.) Philip C. Wilcox

Since the end of the Cold War and the advent of the Arab/Israeli peace process, there has been a growing trend toward consensus in the world in condemning terrorism, irrespective of the political or other motivation behind it. More and more nations, the great majority of the nations indeed, now condemn terrorism without qualification, even though there might be sympathy for the cause motivating the terrorists. It was not always this way. Because of the Cold War and the polarization that it caused and because of the Arab/Israeli conflict, it was very difficult for the international community to deal with terrorism in a collective way. But these geopolitical changes in the world have created a convergence of view and a consensus that terrorism must be addressed and that it is essentially a criminal matter that has to be dealt with severely. As a result, through diplomacy, cooperation among intelligence and law enforcement agencies, and important work done in international organizations, terrorists are increasingly on the defensive.

On one level, international organizations have contributed to this consensus, understanding, and commitment by their declaratory and rhetorical statements. For example, for decades in the United Nations General Assembly, there were annual debates on draft resolutions to address and condemn terrorism. These foundered because of the lack of consensus. You have all heard the phrase "One man's terrorist is another man's freedom fighter." The subtexts of these debates were the ideological divides between the east and west and between Israel and the Arab states. But that has changed. And in 1994, there was a landmark resolution in the General Assembly, which forthrightly condemned terrorism in all of its forms, and called upon nations to combat terrorism in its many manifestations. So the logjam was broken, and thereafter, if I'm not mistaken, this landmark resolution has been reaffirmed annually in the UN General Assembly.

Also on the declarative, rhetorical level, the regional multilateral institutions have spoken out against terrorism in formal resolutions and debates. Ambassador Berhane of Ethiopia has mentioned the work that the Organization of African Unity has done to condemn terrorism and political violence. Others have done the same thing, including the Organization of American States (OAS), the Arab League, and the Organization of the Islamic Conference. In the past it would have been impossible for these organizations to address this issue forthrightly. They have now, and I think that's a great step forward. There have also been subgroups of these organizations, like the Arab League's Association of Ministers in Interior, who have also spoken out and taken action on terrorism.

Second, there has been a movement in international organizations on the more practical level. Most important of all, I think, has been the acceleration of work in the United Nations in drafting and approving 13 international treaties and conventions on various forms of terrorism. Now, this process started as early as 1944. But it has quickened, and there are now 13 of these treaties. Accession of states to these 13 treaties has also accelerated.

They are very important instruments, and they show that the fabric of international law dealing with terrorism has been greatly expanded. Here are the treaties:

- The 1944 Chicago Convention on International Civil Aviation; the 1963 Tokyo Conventions on Offenses Committed Onboard Aircraft;

- The 1970 Hague Convention for the Unlawful Seizure of Aircraft;

- The 1971 Montreal Convention for the Suppression of Unlawful Acts Against Aircraft Safety;

- The 1973 Convention to Prevent and Punish Acts of Terrorism in the Form of Crimes Against Internationally Protected Persons (this deals with acts of kidnapping, hostage taking and extortion);

- The 1979 Convention Against Hostage Taking; the 1979 Convention on Physical Protection of Nuclear Materials;

- A 1988 protocol on the Suppression of Unlawful Acts of Violence at Airports;

- The 1988 International Maritime Organization Convention for Maritime Safety;

• and, The 1991 Convention on the Marking of Plastic Explosives.

Since 1991, there have been two more conventions. One of them on terrorist bombing was adopted in 1998. And in 1999 the General Assembly voted to approve a convention criminalizing terrorist fundraising and financing of terrorist activities. These are important documents.

Many, but not all nations have signed these treaties, and the United States has made a great effort to encourage universal accession. The United States has ratified all but one, I believe.

There are other treaties that are being discussed in the UN. There is a Russian initiative for an International Convention on Nuclear Terrorism. The government of India has proposed a Universal Treaty on Terrorism. The latter is problematical because it would presumably subsume all of these other treaties, which do not attempt to define terrorism in general, but address terrorism in terms of specific criminal acts. So I think the prospect of a universal terrorism treaty at this time is doubtful.

UN specialized agencies have also done a great deal to deter and defend against terrorism. Specifically, the International Civil Aviation Organization, whose regulations on aviation security are universally supported, have made aviation security much more assured. As a result, the number of aircraft hijackings has decreased markedly in recent years.

The International Maritime Organization has also adopted a similar regime, and it is now considering an even tighter regime for maritime safety against acts of terrorism.

The Group of Eight, formerly the Group of Seven, has been very active through its terrorism subgroup over the years and has adopted a host of initiatives for increased international cooperation through diplomatic, intelligence, and law enforcement channels.

The European Union also has a very active subgroup on terrorism, which meets regularly.

The United Nations General Assembly has created a terrorism research cell in Vienna, which is now being staffed and which will bring new intellectual and creative approaches to counter terrorism.

The Organization of American States in our hemisphere has been particularly active. It has held a series of conferences on counter terrorism, and it has recently created and staffed in its headquarters in Washington a Commission on International Crime and Terrorism. The chief of the OAS, Hector Gaviria, the former president of Colombia, has given impetus to this initiative. The charter of the Commission is to promote training in the hemisphere in counter terrorism techniques and methods, and to develop and draft model legislation so that those states in the hemisphere, which have not yet implemented international treaties and conventions, can use this draft law to do so.

Interpol is also a little-known, but very effective, international organization, that among law enforcement agencies identifies and helps national jurisdictions apprehend terrorists. I understand that Interpol is increasing its use of information technology so that its database of terrorist suspects, to which all member governments contribute, can be made more readily available to national law enforcement agencies.

There have also been a host of ad hoc regional international conferences and meetings on terrorism. In Asia, Japan has held such a meeting and the Philippines took a similar initiative several years ago. And there have been others.

I think the declarative and rhetorical approach that international organizations have made and their attention to promoting international law and international treaties have been extremely effective. The basic work of investigating, apprehending, and convicting terrorists, however, has been left to nation-states. International organizations, by and large, have not aspired to taking on this role. The great majority of states believe that, inherently, this work must be done by national jurisdictions, and that we are hardly at the stage where international organizations could assume this responsibility.

There are many reasons for this. Prosecution of terrorists depends heavily on the collection and analysis of sensitive, secret intelligence, and national intelligence agencies are reluctant to hand this intelligence over to international organizations. There is also a lingering concern that international organizations are sometimes affected by politics and might not pursue with enough rigor crimes of terrorism where there were political issues involved.

I believe this is the reason why the International Criminal Court, a treaty which was drafted last year, has not been given jurisdiction over terrorist crimes. When the international criminal court was being discussed, the United States for one opposed giving the court jurisdiction over terrorist crimes. As you know, in the end the United States did not accede to the treaty in its final form.

Some small states, which lack internal capabilities to fight terrorism, would like to see a more operational responsibility given to multilateral organizations. But by and large that has not happened. Overall, there isn't any great tension between the respective roles of international organizations and nation-states in this area.

To conclude, much has been done by the community of nations acting collectively to raise the profile of the menace of terrorism, increase understanding, and enhance the collective will to go after terrorists. Nevertheless, the actual work of counter terrorism is more often than not done by states acting individually, or where two or more states are involved, through bilateral, diplomatic, law enforcement, and intelligence cooperation.

One more area where an international organization has acted effectively against terrorism, was a resolution of the United Nations Security Council condemning the suspected bombing of Pan American flight 103 by agents of the government of Libya. That was a landmark decision, the first time I believe that the Security Council has criminalized an action by a nation-state in support of terrorism. Finally, after many years, the rule of law and justice will be served. Thank you.

Prof. Christopher C. Joyner

The United Nations provides a very important vehicle and instrument to be used by the United States and all states in their efforts to combat the scourge of terrorism. In my view, the United Nations is the major forum in which governments have met over the last three decades to negotiate new norms and specifically to negotiate new agreements that can be used to outlaw and combat terrorist activities.

The preeminent deficiency in the United Nations efforts has been the inability to come to a resolute definition of what constitutes terrorism. That point has been made and needs to be made again. Because if you read the debates in the Sixth Legal Committee of the General Assembly, in which many of these conventions are being thrashed out, there is a profound concern by the delegates of the need to define terrorism. This is especially so in order to distinguish "terrorist acts" from national liberation struggles and the concern of legitimate efforts to throw off foreign domination. The point here, though, is that because of this definitional dilemma, the United Nations, as a consensus building organization, has been unable to come to grips with a single convention aimed at establishing legal controls for terrorism at large.

What has the United Nations done? Well, the United Nations has adopted a piecemeal approach towards dealing with terrorism by negotiating separate conventions aimed at suppressing a number of acts and activities that most of us would agree are terrorist in nature. Interestingly enough, the term "terrorism" or the crime of terrorism is not defined, even though you will see the term in the title of a number of these conventions.

There are thirteen prominent United Nations conventions which have been negotiated thus far. Not all of them are in force. The last two, in particular, are noticeably deficient in terms of parties. But the point is that there has been a profound contribution to international law and to international state coordination of efforts in outlawing acts which we all would agree are terrorist in nature. If you also look at these particular conventions (International Civil Aeronautics Organization (ICAO) conventions; the International Maritime Organization (IMO) maritime conventions; the protection of international diplomatic agents; the taking of hostages convention; safeguarding of nuclear materials) all of these, in concert, provide an international regime to combat terrorism.

It is not a satisfactory regime; it is not a sufficient regime; but it is a framework for dealing with terrorism on an ad hoc basis, and the United Nations gets credit for this. You can also give credit to individual member states that promoted many of these conventions, the United States being a leader in this regard. The United States has ratified all but two, I think, of these conventions.

But the fact remains that there is a regime in place for dealing with international terrorists, and the regime comes from the United Nations. There is an ad hoc committee, which has been in existence since 1996, specifically devoted to terrorism. It is this ad hoc committee which has been the sponsor and drafter, through the Sixth Legal Committee of the General Assembly, for the last two major conventions: A 1997 convention for the suppression of terrorist bombings and the 1999 convention for the suppression of the financing of terrorists. There is also on the agenda, an international convention on the suppression of nuclear attacks, nuclear bombings.

The most recent instrument to be adopted by the United Nations dealing with terrorism is the Convention on the Suppression of Terrorist Financing. It is an instrument in which states who become parties will have to make provision in their own criminal laws that such financing is unlawful; that parties will have to confiscate assets that are being used for terrorist purposes; and that these assets will be shared amongst the parties, as well as the victims of any terrorist acts that are committed. There are twenty-eight provisions in this instrument, and what the convention does is to use the eleven main conventions adopted by the United Nations as the crimes or offenses covered by the convention. The financing of any criminal activities associated with the eleven previous conventions would be an offense under this Convention on the Financing of Terrorism. The convention will enter into force once it has twenty-two ratifications.

Let me give you some highlights of what this convention does. I do this not to regurgitate a legal instrument, but rather to emphasize to you the sophistication which the negotiators are using in order to ensure apprehension, prosecution, and punishment of persons who are accused of this offense. The offense within the convention is defined as, "any person who collects funds or assists in the collection of funds or has a knowledge of such collection of funds, which are used in part or in full to carry out any of the offenses in the eleven conventions." Article 3 ensures respect for sovereignty of each state. In Article 3 there is the assertion that territorial jurisdiction will apply to each state if the crime is committed by a national of a state affecting only that state. Article 5 would ensure that each state that becomes a party would implement this convention through the passage of municipal law to effect the provisions of this convention and to implement them accordingly.

Article 7 provides the basis of jurisdiction over any potential offenders. This is a very interesting provision because it accepts the principle of territoriality. That is, if an offense is committed within the territory of the state, jurisdiction will apply. It sets out the principle of nationality, that is, if the offense is committed by the national of a state. It also sets out the principle of universal jurisdiction. That is, any state, anywhere, any time, may apprehend any offender whether or not that crime was committed on that state's territory. So, universal jurisdiction is supplied in this convention. And, again, in Article 7, Paragraph 6, it is reaffirmed "without prejudice to the norms of general international law, that this convention does not exclude the exercise of any criminal jurisdiction established by a state party in accordance with this domestic law." There is also provided for in this convention an article to compensate victims or families of victims for terrorist acts, and this compensation would accrue from assets, monies, or funds that have been seized or frozen because they have been used to support terrorism.

Most importantly, there is an "extradite or prosecute" provision in this convention. Article 10 asserts that, "If a government who has jurisdiction over a potential offender does not prosecute that person, then the person must be extradited." Conversely, if the person is not to be extradited, then the person must be prosecuted by that state.

Last, but not least, Article 14 excludes the political offense exception. There is an overt statement in Article 14 that says, "No offense in this convention, for the purposes of extradition, may be excused on the basis of a political offense." So this furnishes a very important safeguard against a terrorist being able to establish safe haven or refuge on the basis of a political offense exception, if indeed he is apprehended. In the case of a dispute between parties, there are provisions for dispute settlement through mandatory arbitration, and if that does not work, then through submission to the International Court of Justice.

In conclusion, let me say that the United Nations is not a panacea for controlling or suppressing terrorist activities, but it is the most universal of international organizations. It is the world forum that brings together 189 governments and provides an opportunity to articulate legal norms and to construct international conventions designed to suppress terrorist activities. To the extent that has been possible thus far, the successful record to make the conventions work really belongs to national governments. We can agree on the terms. To make them work effectively depends on the political will of national governments.

My last point—the most recent convention that was adopted by the General Assembly and opened for signature on January 10th of 2000, attracted 18 states as signatories. As yet, there are no parties. I just want to mention a eight of those signatories to you because they stand out for one reason or another as victims of terrorist acts given their history: Algeria, Canada, Greece, Russian Federation, Sri Lanka, Sudan, United Kingdom, and the United States.

If you read the debates on this convention and the other conventions, it is very interesting to note which states were most adamant in advocating the protection of the struggle for national liberation, and for insisting upon a definition of terrorism. Cuba, Syria, and Libya in every debate had their representatives make strikingly similar statements advocating the need for a clear definition of terrorism and also advocating the need to insulate or distinguish that definition from the national struggle against foreign domination and occupation.

II.
Selected Documents

DOCUMENT No. I

CALIFORNIA

ARTICLE 3.6
Title 11.5

TERRORIST THREATS

§ 422. Elements of offense; punishment; "immediate family" defined

Any person who willfully threatens to commit a crime which will result in death or great bodily injury to another person, with the specific intent that the statement, *made verbally, in writing, or by means of an electronic communication device*, is to be taken as a threat, even if there is no intent of actually carrying it out, which, on its face and under the circumstances in which it is made, is so unequivocal, unconditional, immediate, and specific as to convey to the person threatened, a gravity of purpose and an immediate prospect of execution of the threat, and thereby causes that person reasonably to be in sustained fear for his or her own safety or for his or her immediate family's safety, shall be punished by imprisonment in the county jail not to exceed one year, or by imprisonment in the state prison.

For the purposes of this section, "immediate family" means any spouse whether by marriage or not, parent, child, any person related by consanguinity or affinity within the second degree, or any other person who regularly resides in the household, or who, within the prior six months, regularly resided in the household.

"Electronic communication device" includes, but is not limited to, telephones, cellular telephones, computers, video recorders, fax machines, or pagers. "Electronic communication" has the same meaning as the term defined in Subsection 12 of Section 2510 of Title 18 of the United States Code.

VICTIM COMPENSATION

California law provides for the compensation of victims of crime. Cal. Gov't. Code §§ 13960 through 13969.4 (West 1999). The term "Crime" is defined to include "...an act of terrorism, as defined in Section 2331 of Title 18 of the United States Code, committed against a resident of the state, whether or not the act occurs within the state." § 13960 (c).

DOCUMENT No. 2

ILLINOIS

ANTI-TERRORISM PROVISIONS

5/29C-5. Definitions

§ 29C-5. Definitions. In this Article:

"International terrorism" means activities that: (i) involve a violent act of acts, perpetrated by a private person or non-governmental entity, dangerous to human life that would be a felony under the laws of the State of Illinois if committed within the jurisdiction of the State of Illinois; and (ii) occur outside the United States; and (iii) are intended to intimidate or coerce a civilian population, influence the policy of a government by intimidation or coercion, or affect the conduct of government by assassination or kidnapping.

"Material support or resources" means currency or other financial securities, financial services, lodging, training, safe houses, false documentation or identification, communications equipment, facilities, weapons, lethal substances, explosives, personnel, transportation, and other physical assets.

"Charitable organization", "professional fund raiser" and "professional solicitor" have the meanings ascribed to them in Section 1 of the Solicitation for Charity Act.

5/29C-10. Solicitation of material support or resources in support of international terrorism

§ 29-10. Solicitation of material support or resources in support of international terrorism
  (a) A person, charitable organization, professional fund raiser, or professional solicitor commits solicitation of material support or resources in support of international terrorism when he, she, or the charitable organization raises, solicits, or collects material support or resources intending that the material support or resources will be used, in whole or in part, to plan, prepare, carry out, or escape from an act or acts of international terrorism.
  (b) Sentence. Solicitation of material support or resources in support of international terrorism is a Class 1 felony.

5/29C-15. Providing material support or resources for international terrorism

§ 29C-15. Providing material support or resources for international terrorism

(a) A person commits providing material support or resources for international terrorism when he or she provides material support or resources to a person or an organization, intending that the material support or resources will be used, in whole or in part, to plan, prepare, carry out, or escape from an act or acts of international terrorism.

(b) Investigations.

    (1) Within this State, an investigation may be initiated or continued under this Section only when the facts reasonably indicate that:

        (A) in the case of an individual, the individual knowingly or intentionally engages or has engaged in the violation of this or any other criminal law of this State; and

        (B) in the case of a group of individuals, the group knowingly or intentionally engages or has engaged in the violation of this or any other criminal law of this State.

    (2) Activities protected by the First Amendment. An investigation may not be initiated or continued under this Section based on activities protected by the First Amendment to the United States Constitution, including expressions of support or the provision of financial support for the nonviolent political, religious, philosophical, or ideological goals or beliefs of any person or group.

(c) Sentence. Providing material support or resources for international terrorism is a Class 1 felony.

DOCUMENT No. 3

OHIO

<u>TAXES</u>

[§ 5747.02.3] § 5747.023 Exemption for armed forces member killed as a result of combat zone service; certain persons killed outside U.S. in a terroristic or military action.

(A) Any individual who dies while in active service as a member of the armed forces or the United States, if such death occurred while serving in a combat zone or as a result of wounds, disease, or injury incurred while so serving, shall be exempt from taxes as follows:

  (1) Any taxes imposed by this chapter or Chapter 5748. of the Revised Code for taxable year commencing after 1990 if the individual is exempted by division (a)(1) of section 692 of the Internal Revenue Code from federal income taxes for such taxable year;

  (2) Any taxes imposed under this chapter or Chapter 5748. of the Revised Code for taxable years preceding those specified in division (A)(1) of this section if the taxes are unpaid at the date of the individual's death and the individual would be exempted by division (a)(2) of section 692 of the Internal Revenue Code from paying such taxes if they were unpaid federal income taxes.

(B) An individual who dies after 1990 while a military or civilian employee of the United States, if such death occurs as a result of wounds or injury incurred while the individual was a military or civilian employee of the United States and also incurred outside the United States in a terroristic or military action, shall be exempt from any taxes imposed by this chapter or Chapter 5748. of the Revised Code for a taxable year if the individual is exempted by division (c) of section 692 of the Internal Revenue Code from federal income taxes for such taxable year.

(C) If an individual subject to this section is included in a joint return for federal income tax purposes, the individual also shall be included in a joint return for purposes of this chapter and Chapter 5748. of the Revised Code, and the effect of any exemption under this section on such joint tax liability shall be determined in a manner consistent with the determination of the effect of any exemption under section 692 of the Internal Revenue Code on such joint tax liability.

(D) As used in this section, "taxes" includes penalties and interest.

DOCUMENT No. 4

SOUTH DAKOTA

<u>DESTRUCTIVE DEVICES</u>

22-14A-4. Sale, transportation, or possession of destructive device as felony—Increased penalty for prior violent crime conviction.

Any person who knowingly sells, offers for sale, transports or possesses any destructive device is guilty of a Class 4 felony. If such person has been previously convicted of a crime of violence in this state or elsewhere, he is guilty of a Class 3 felony.

22-14A-5. Carrying or placing explosive or device on vehicle or in baggage—Felony

Any person who, with intent to injure or to threaten to injure any person or property:
  (1) Carries any explosive or destructive device on any vessel, aircraft, motor vehicle or other vehicle that transports passengers for hire;
  (2) Places or carries any explosive or destructive device, while on board any such vessel, aircraft, motor vehicle, or other vehicle, in any hand baggage, roll or other container with intent to conceal the same;
  (3) Places any explosive or destructive device in any baggage which is later checked with any common carrier;
is guilty of a Class 2 felony.

22-14A-6. Possession of explosive or device with intent to injure, intimidate or destroy property as felony.

Any person who has in his possession any explosive or destructive device under circumstances not enumerated in § 22-14A-5, with intent to injure, intimidate, or terrify any person, or with intent to wrongfully injure or destroy any property is guilty of a Class 3 felony.

22-14A-11. Intentional use of device or explosive to cause bodily harm as felony.

Any person who explodes or ignites any destructive device or explosive with intent to cause bodily harm and which results in bodily harm is guilty of a Class 2 felony.

22-14A-13. Unauthorized possession of substances with intent to make destructive device as felony.

Any person who possesses any substance, material, or any combination of the substances or materials, with the intent to make a destructive device without first obtaining a permit from the department of public safety to make such device, is guilty of a Class 5 felony.

22-14A-16. Armed forces, law enforcement agencies, and licensed sellers or users of explosives and destructive devices exempt.

This chapter shall not apply to the armed forces of the United States, the national guard, any law enforcement agency or any officer, agent, employee or member thereof acting in a lawful capacity and any person possessing a valid seller's permit or user's permit from the United States federal government for explosive and destructive devices.

22-14A-18. Use of explosive or device to destroy another's property as felony— Exception.

Any person who intentionally destroys or attempts to destroy by the use of any explosive or destructive device, any property real or personal, not the property of such person, although the same is done under such circumstances as not to endanger the life or safety of any human being, is guilty of a Class 4 felony. This section shall not apply to any property destroyed under the direction of any fire fighter or any law enforcement officer of any municipality to prevent the spread of fire.

22-14A-19. Use of explosive or device to endanger human life or safely as felony.

Any person who intentionally, by the use of an explosive or destructive device, destroys or inures the whole or any part of any occupied or unoccupied structure, motor vehicle, street, highway, railway, bridge, dam, dyke or other structure, by means of which the life or safety of any human being is endangered, is guilty of a Class 3 felony.

22-14A-20. Placement of explosive or device as to endanger human life or safety.

Any person who takes into, upon, under, against, or near to any occupied or unoccupied structure, motor vehicle, street, highway, railway, bridge, dam, dyke or other structure, any explosive or destructive device, with intent to destroy or injure the whole or any part thereof under the circumstances that if such intent were accomplished, human life or safety would be endangered thereby, although no damage is done, is guilty of a Class 4 felony.

22-14A-21. Possession of registered or licensed destructive devices permitted.

Any person may possess destructive devices that are registered with, or licensed by, the state or federal government pursuant to law.

22-14A-22. Falsely reporting a bomb as felony—Restitution Minor to perform public service.

Any person who makes a false report, with intent to deceive, mislead, or otherwise misinform any person, concerning the placing or planting of any bomb, dynamite, explosive, or destructive device, is guilty of falsely reporting a bomb. Falsely reporting a bomb is a Class 6 felony. Any person found guilty of falsely reporting a bomb shall pay restitution for any expense incurred as a result of the crime. The person is also civilly liable for any injury to person or property from the false report and any costs related to responding to the false report. If the person making the false report prohibited by this section is a minor, the court, in addition to such other disposition as the court may impose, shall require the minor to perform at least fifty hours of public service unless tried as an adult.

DOCUMENT No. 5

TITLE 18, UNITED STATES CODE, CRIMES AND CRIMINAL PROCEDURE

PART I - CRIMES

Chapter 10. Biological weapons

Sec. 175. Prohibitions with respect to biological weapons

- (a) In General. - Whoever knowingly develops, produces, stockpiles, transfers, acquires, retains, or possesses any biological agent, toxin, or delivery system for use as a weapon, or knowingly assists a foreign state or any organization to do so, or attempts, threatens, or conspires to do the same, shall be fined under this title or imprisoned for life or any term of years, or both. There is extraterritorial Federal jurisdiction over an offense under this section committed by or against a national of the United States.
- (b) Definition. - For purposes of this section, the term "for use as a weapon" does not include the development, production, transfer, acquisition, retention, or possession of any biological agent, toxin, or delivery system for prophylactic, protective, or other peaceful purposes.

Sec. 175a. Requests for military assistance to enforce prohibition in certain emergencies

The Attorney General may request the Secretary of Defense to provide assistance under section 382 of title 10 in support of Department of Justice activities relating to the enforcement of section 175 of this title in an emergency situation involving a biological weapon of mass destruction. The authority to make such a request may be exercised by another official of the Department of Justice in accordance with section 382(f)(2) of title 10.

Sec. 176. Seizure, forfeiture, and destruction

- (a) In General. - (1) Except as provided in paragraph (2), the Attorney General may request the issuance, in the same manner as provided for a search warrant, of a warrant authorizing the seizure of any biological agent, toxin, or delivery system that -
  - o (A) exists by reason of conduct prohibited under section 175 of

this title; or

- o (B) is of a type or in a quantity that under the circumstances has no apparent justification for prophylactic, protective, or other peaceful purposes.

  § (2) In exigent circumstances, seizure and destruction of any biological agent, toxin, or delivery system described in subparagraphs (A) and (B) of paragraph (1) may be made upon probable cause without the necessity for a warrant.

- (b) Procedure. - Property seized pursuant to subsection (a) shall be forfeited to the United States after notice to potential claimants and an opportunity for a hearing. At such hearing, the Government shall bear the burden of persuasion by a preponderance of the evidence. Except as inconsistent herewith, the same procedures and provisions of law relating to a forfeiture under the customs laws shall extend to a seizure or forfeiture under this section. The Attorney General may provide for the destruction or other appropriate disposition of any biological agent, toxin, or delivery system seized and forfeited pursuant to this section.

- (c) Affirmative Defense. - It is an affirmative defense against a forfeiture under subsection (a)(1)(B) of this section that -

  - o (1) such biological agent, toxin, or delivery system is for a prophylactic, protective, or other peaceful purpose; and
    (2) such biological agent, toxin, or delivery system, is of a type and quantity reasonable for that purpose.

Sec. 177. Injunctions

- (a) In General. - The United States may obtain in a civil action an injunction against -

  - o (1) the conduct prohibited under section 175 of this title;
  - o (2) the preparation, solicitation, attempt, threat, or conspiracy to engage in conduct prohibited under section 175 of this title; or
  - o (3) the development, production, stockpiling, transferring, acquisition, retention, or possession, or the attempted development, production, stockpiling, transferring, acquisition, retention, or possession of any biological agent, toxin, or delivery system of a type or in a quantity that under the circumstances has no apparent justification for prophylactic, protective, or other peaceful purposes.

- (b) Affirmative Defense. - It is an affirmative defense against an injunction under subsection (a)(3) of this section that -

  - o (1) the conduct sought to be enjoined is for a prophylactic, protective, or other peaceful purpose; and
  - o (2) such biological agent, toxin, or delivery system is of a type and quantity reasonable for that purpose.

Sec. 178. Definitions

As used in this chapter -

- (1) the term "biological agent" means any micro-organism, virus, infectious substance, or biological product that may be engineered as a result of biotechnology, or any naturally occurring or bioengineered component of any such microorganism, virus, infectious substance, or biological product, capable of causing -
  - o (A) death, disease, or other biological malfunction in a human, an animal, a plant, or another living organism;
  - o (B) deterioration of food, water, equipment, supplies, or material of any kind; or
  - o (C) deleterious alteration of the environment;
- (2) the term "toxin" means the toxic material of plants, animals, microorganisms, viruses, fungi, or infectious substances, or a recombinant molecule, whatever its origin or method of production, including -
  - o (A) any poisonous substance or biological product that may be engineered as a result of biotechnology produced by a living organism; or
  - o (B) any poisonous isomer or biological product, homolog, or derivative of such a substance;
- (3) the term "delivery system" means -
  - o (A) any apparatus, equipment, device, or means of delivery specifically designed to deliver or disseminate a biological agent, toxin, or vector; or
  - o (B) any vector;
- (4) the term "vector" means a living organism, or molecule, including a recombinant molecule, or biological product that may be engineered as a result of biotechnology, capable of carrying a biological agent or toxin to a host; and
  (5) the term "national of the United States" has the meaning prescribed in section 101(a)(22) of the Immigration and Nationality Act (8 U.S.C. 1101(a)(22)).

Chapter 11B. Chemical Weapons

Sec. 229. Prohibited activities

- (a) Unlawful Conduct. - Except as provided in subsection (b), it shall be unlawful for any person knowingly -
  - o (1) to develop, produce, otherwise acquire, transfer directly or indirectly, receive, stockpile, retain, own, possess, or use, or threaten to use, any chemical weapon; or
  - o (2) to assist or induce, in any way, any person to violate

paragraph (1), or to attempt or conspire to violate paragraph (1).

- (b) Exempted Agencies and Persons. -
  - o (1) In general. - Subsection (a) does not apply to the retention, ownership, possession, transfer, or receipt of a chemical weapon by a department, agency, or other entity of the United States, or by a person described in paragraph (2), pending destruction of the weapon.
  - o (2) Exempted persons. - A person referred to in paragraph (1) is -
    - § (A) any person, including a member of the Armed Forces of the United States, who is authorized by law or by an appropriate officer of the United States to retain, own, possess, transfer, or receive the chemical weapon; or
    - § (B) in an emergency situation, any otherwise nonculpable person if the person is attempting to destroy or seize the weapon.
- (c) Jurisdiction. - Conduct prohibited by subsection (a) is within the jurisdiction of the United States if the prohibited conduct -
  - o (1) takes place in the United States;
  - o (2) takes place outside of the United States and is committed by a national of the United States;
  - o (3) is committed against a national of the United States while the national is outside the United States; or
  - o (4) is committed against any property that is owned, leased, or used by the United States or by any department or agency of the United States, whether the property is within or outside the United States.

Sec. 229A. Penalties

- (a) Criminal Penalties. -
  - o (1) In general. - Any person who violates section 229 of this title shall be fined under this title, or imprisoned for any term of years, or both.
  - o (2) Death penalty. - Any person who violates section 229 of this title and by whose action the death of another person is the result shall be punished by death or imprisoned for life.
- (b) Civil Penalties. -
  - o (1) In general. - The Attorney General may bring a civil action in the appropriate United States district court against any person who violates section 229 of this title and, upon proof of such violation by a preponderance of the evidence, such person shall be subject to pay a civil penalty in an amount not to

exceed $100,000 for each such violation.

o   (2) Relation to other proceedings. - The imposition of a civil penalty under this subsection does not preclude any other criminal or civil statutory, common law, or administrative remedy, which is available by law to the United States or any other person.

- (c) Reimbursement of Costs. - The court shall order any person convicted of an offense under subsection (a) to reimburse the United States for any expenses incurred by the United States incident to the seizure, storage, handling, transportation, and destruction or other disposition of any property that was seized in connection with an investigation of the commission of the offense by that person. A person ordered to reimburse the United States for expenses under this subsection shall be jointly and severally liable for such expenses with each other person, if any, who is ordered under this subsection to reimburse the United States for the same expenses.

Sec. 229B. Criminal forfeitures; destruction of weapons

- (a) Property Subject to Criminal Forfeiture. - Any person convicted under section 229A(a) shall forfeit to the United States irrespective of any provision of State law -
    - o   (1) any property, real or personal, owned, possessed, or used by a person involved in the offense;
    - o   (2) any property constituting, or derived from, and proceeds the person obtained, directly or indirectly, as the result of such violation; and
    - o   (3) any of the property used in any manner or part, to commit, or to facilitate the commission of, such violation. The court, in imposing sentence on such person, shall order, in addition to any other sentence imposed pursuant to section 229A(a), that the person forfeit to the United States all property described in this subsection. In lieu of a fine otherwise authorized by section 229A(a), a defendant who derived profits or other proceeds from an offense may be fined not more than twice the gross profits or other proceeds.
- (b) Procedures. -
    - o   (1) General. - Property subject to forfeiture under this section, any seizure and disposition thereof, and any administrative or judicial proceeding in relation thereto, shall be governed by subsections (b) through (p) of section 413 of the Comprehensive Drug Abuse Prevention and Control Act of 1970 (21 U.S.C. 853), except that any reference under those subsections to
        - ▪ (A) "this subchapter or subchapter II" shall be deemed to be a reference to section 229A(a); and
        - ▪ (B) "subsection (a)" shall be deemed to be a reference to

subsection (a) of this section.
- o (2) Temporary restraining orders. -
  - (A) In general. - For the purposes of forfeiture proceedings under this section, a temporary restraining order may be entered upon application of the United States without notice or opportunity for a hearing when an information or indictment has not yet been filed with respect to the property, if, in addition to the circumstances described in section 413(e)(2) of the Comprehensive Drug Abuse Prevention and Control Act of 1970 (21 U.S.C. 853(e)(2)), the United States demonstrates that there is probable cause to believe that the property with respect to which the order is sought would, in the event of conviction, be subject to forfeiture under this section and exigent circumstances exist that place the life or health of any person in danger.
  - (B) Warrant of seizure. - If the court enters a temporary restraining order under this paragraph, it shall also issue a warrant authorizing the seizure of such property.
  - (C) Applicable procedures. - The procedures and time limits applicable to temporary restraining orders under section 413(e)(2) and (3) of the Comprehensive Drug Abuse Prevention and Control Act of 1970 (21 U.S.C. 853(e)(2) and (3)) shall apply to temporary restraining orders under this paragraph.
- (c) Affirmative Defense. - It is an affirmative defense against a forfeiture under subsection (b) that the property -
  - o (1) is for a purpose not prohibited under the Chemical Weapons Convention; and
  - o (2) is of a type and quantity that under the circumstances is consistent with that purpose.
- (d) Destruction or Other Disposition. - The Attorney General shall provide for the destruction or other appropriate disposition of any chemical weapon seized and forfeited pursuant to this section.
- (e) Assistance. - The Attorney General may request the head of any agency of the United States to assist in the handling, storage, transportation, or destruction of property seized under this section.
- (f) Owner Liability. - The owner or possessor of any property seized under this section shall be liable to the United States for any expenses incurred incident to the seizure, including any expenses relating to the handling, storage, transportation, and destruction or other disposition of the seized property.

Sec. 229C. Individual self-defense devices

Nothing in this chapter shall be construed to prohibit any individual self-defense device, including those using a pepper spray or chemical mace.

Sec. 229D. Injunctions

The United States may obtain in a civil action an injunction against -

- (1) the conduct prohibited under section 229 or 229C of this title; or
- (2) the preparation or solicitation to engage in conduct prohibited under section 229 or 229D of this title.

Sec. 229E. Requests for military assistance to enforce prohibition in certain emergencies

The Attorney General may request the Secretary of Defense to provide assistance under section 382 of title 10 in support of Department of Justice activities relating to the enforcement of section 229 of this title in an emergency situation involving a chemical weapon. The authority to make such a request may be exercised by another official of the Department of Justice in accordance with section 382(f)(2) of title 10.

Sec. 229F. Definitions

In this chapter:

- (1) Chemical weapon. - The term "chemical weapon" means the following, together or separately:
    - o (A) A toxic chemical and its precursors, except where intended for a purpose not prohibited under this chapter as long as the type and quantity is consistent with such a purpose.
    - o (B) A munition or device, specifically designed to cause death or other harm through toxic properties of those toxic chemicals specified in subparagraph (A), which would be released as a result of the employment of such munition or device.
    - o (C) Any equipment specifically designed for use directly in connection with the employment of munitions or devices specified in subparagraph (B).
- (2) Chemical weapons convention; convention. - The terms "Chemical Weapons Convention" and "Convention" mean the Convention on the Prohibition of the Development, Production, Stockpiling and Use of Chemical Weapons and on Their Destruction, opened for signature on January 13, 1993.
- (3) Key component of a binary or multicomponent chemical system. - The term "key component of a binary or multicomponent chemical system" means the precursor which plays the most important role in determining the toxic properties of the final product and reacts rapidly with other chemicals in the binary or multicomponent system.
- (4) National of the united states. - The term "national of the United States" has the same meaning given such term in section 101(a)(22) of the

Immigration and Nationality Act (8 U.S.C. 1101(a)(22)).
- (5) Person. - The term "person", except as otherwise provided, means any individual, corporation, partnership, firm, association, trust, estate, public or private institution, any State or any political subdivision thereof, or any political entity within a State, any foreign government or nation or any agency, instrumentality or political subdivision of any such government or nation, or other entity located in the United States.
- (6) Precursor. -
    o (A) In general. - The term "precursor" means any chemical reactant which takes part at any stage in the production by whatever method of a toxic chemical. The term includes any key component of a binary or multicomponent chemical system.
    o (B) List of precursors. - Precursors which have been identified for the application of verification measures under Article VI of the Convention are listed in schedules contained in the Annex on Chemicals of the Chemical Weapons Convention.
- (7) Purposes not prohibited by this chapter. - The term "purposes not prohibited by this chapter" means the following:
    o (A) Peaceful purposes. - Any peaceful purpose related to an industrial, agricultural, research, medical, or pharmaceutical activity or other activity.
    o (B) Protective purposes. - Any purpose directly related to protection against toxic chemicals and to protection against chemical weapons.
    o (C) Unrelated military purposes. - Any military purpose of the United States that is not connected with the use of a chemical weapon or that is not dependent on the use of the toxic or poisonous properties of the chemical weapon to cause death or other harm.
    o (D) Law enforcement purposes. - Any law enforcement purpose, including any domestic riot control purpose and including imposition of capital punishment.
- (8) Toxic chemical. -
    o (A) In general. - The term "toxic chemical" means any chemical which through its chemical action on life processes can cause death, temporary incapacitation or permanent harm to humans or animals. The term includes all such chemicals, regardless of their origin or of their method of production, and regardless of whether they are produced in facilities, in munitions or elsewhere.
    o (B) List of toxic chemicals. - Toxic chemicals which have been identified for the application of verification measures under Article VI of the Convention are listed in schedules contained in the Annex on Chemicals of the Chemical Weapons Convention.

- (9) United states. - The term "United States" means the several States of the United States, the District of Columbia, and the commonwealths, territories, and possessions of the United States and includes all places under the jurisdiction or control of the United States, including -
  - o (A) any of the places within the provisions of paragraph (41) of section 40102 of title 49, United States Code;
  - o (B) any civil aircraft of the United States or public aircraft, as such terms are defined in paragraphs (17) and (37), respectively, of section 40102 of title 49, United States Code; and
  - o (C) any vessel of the United States, as such term is defined in section 3(b) of the Maritime Drug Enforcement Act, as amended (46 U.S.C., App. sec. 1903(b)).

Chapter 55. Kidnapping

Sec. 1203. Hostage taking

- (a) Except as provided in subsection (b) of this section, whoever, whether inside or outside the United States, seizes or detains and threatens to kill, to injure, or to continue to detain another person in order to compel a third person or a governmental organization to do or abstain from doing any act as an explicit or implicit condition for the release of the person detained, or attempts or conspires to do so, shall be punished by imprisonment for any term of years or for life and, if the death of any person results, shall be punished by death or life imprisonment.
- (b)
  - o (1) It is not an offense under this section if the conduct required for the offense occurred outside the United States unless -
    - (A) the offender or the person seized or detained is a national of the United States;
    - (B) the offender is found in the United States; or
    - (C) the governmental organization sought to be compelled is the Government of the United States.
  - o (2) It is not an offense under this section if the conduct required for the offense occurred inside the United States, each alleged offender and each person seized or detained are nationals of the United States, and each alleged offender is found in the United States, unless the governmental organization sought to be compelled is the Government of the United States.
- (c) As used in this section, the term "national of the United States" has the meaning given such term in section 101(a)(22) of the Immigration and Nationality Act (8 U.S.C. 1101(a)(22)).
    - (A) whether joint or sole (and includes visiting rights); and

Chapter 113B. Terrorism

Sec. 2331. Definitions

As used in this chapter -

- (1) the term "international terrorism" means activities that

    o (A) involve violent acts or acts dangerous to human life that are a violation of the criminal laws of the United States or of any State, or that would be a criminal violation if committed within the jurisdiction of the United States or of any State;
    o (B) appear to be intended -
        - (i) to intimidate or coerce a civilian population;
        - (ii) to influence the policy of a government by intimidation or coercion; or
        - (iii) to affect the conduct of a government by assassination or kidnapping; and
    o (C) occur primarily outside the territorial jurisdiction of the United States, or transcend national boundaries in terms of the means by which they are accomplished, the persons they appear intended to intimidate or coerce, or the locale in which their perpetrators operate or seek asylum;
- (2) the term "national of the United States" has the meaning given such term in section 101(a)(22) of the Immigration and Nationality Act;
- (3) the term "person" means any individual or entity capable of holding a legal or beneficial interest in property; and
- (4) the term "act of war" means any act occurring in the course of -
    o (A) declared war;
    o (B) armed conflict, whether or not war has been declared, between two or more nations; or
    o (C) armed conflict between military forces of any origin.

Sec. 2332. Criminal penalties

- (a) Homicide. - Whoever kills a national of the United States, while such national is outside the United States, shall -
    o (1) if the killing is murder (as defined in section 1111(a)), be fined under this title, punished by death or imprisonment for any term of years or for life, or both;
    o (2) if the killing is a voluntary manslaughter as defined in section 1112(a) of this title, be fined under this title or imprisoned not more than ten years, or both; and
        (3) if the killing is an involuntary manslaughter as defined in section 1112(a) of this title, be fined under this title or imprisoned not more than three years, or both.
- (b) Attempt or Conspiracy With Respect to Homicide. - Whoever outside

the United States attempts to kill, or engages in a conspiracy to kill, a national of the United States shall -

- o (1) in the case of an attempt to commit a killing that is a murder as defined in this chapter, be fined under this title or imprisoned not more than 20 years, or both; and
- o (2) in the case of a conspiracy by two or more persons to commit a killing that is a murder as defined in section 1111(a) of this title, if one or more of such persons do any overt act to effect the object of the conspiracy, be fined under this title or imprisoned for any term of years or for life, or both so fined and so imprisoned.

- (c) Other Conduct. - Whoever outside the United States engages in physical violence -
  - o (1) with intent to cause serious bodily injury to a national of the United States; or
  - o (2) with the result that serious bodily injury is caused to a national of the United States; shall be fined under this title or imprisoned not more than ten years, or both.

- (d) Limitation on Prosecution. - No prosecution for any offense described in this section shall be undertaken by the United States except on written certification of the Attorney General or the highest ranking subordinate of the Attorney General with responsibility for criminal prosecutions that, in the judgment of the certifying official, such offense was intended to coerce, intimidate, or retaliate against a government or a civilian population.

Sec. 2332a. Use of certain weapons of mass destruction

- (a) Offense Against a National of the United States or Within the United States. - A person who, without lawful authority, uses, threatens, or attempts or conspires to use, a weapon of mass destruction (other than a chemical weapon as that term is defined in section 229F), including any biological agent, toxin, or vector (as those terms are defined in section 178)
  -
  - o (1) against a national of the United States while such national is outside of the United States;
  - o (2) against any person within the United States, and the results of such use affect interstate or foreign commerce or, in the case of a threat, attempt, or conspiracy, would have affected interstate or foreign commerce; or
  - o (3) against any property that is owned, leased or used by the United States or by any department or agency of the United States, whether the property is within or outside of the United States, shall be imprisoned for any term of years or for life, and if death results, shall be punished by death or imprisoned for any term of years or for life.

- (b) Offense by National of the United States Outside of the United States.

- Any national of the United States who, without lawful authority, uses, or threatens, attempts, or conspires to use, a weapon of mass destruction (other than a chemical weapon (as that term is defined in section 229F)) outside of the United States shall be imprisoned for any term of years or for life, and if death results, shall be punished by death, or by imprisonment for any term of years or for life.

- (c) Definitions. - For purposes of this section -
  - o (1) the term "national of the United States" has the meaning given in section 101(a)(22) of the Immigration and Nationality Act (8 U.S.C. 1101(a)(22)); and
    (2) the term "weapon of mass destruction" means -
    - (A) any destructive device as defined in section 921 of this title;
    - (B) any weapon that is designed or intended to cause death or serious bodily injury through the release, dissemination, or impact of toxic or poisonous chemicals, or their precursors;
    - (C) any weapon involving a disease organism; or
    - (D) any weapon that is designed to release radiation or radioactivity at a level dangerous to human life.

Sec. 2332b. Acts of terrorism transcending national boundaries

- (a) Prohibited Acts. -
  - o (1) Offenses. - Whoever, involving conduct transcending national boundaries and in a circumstance described in subsection (b) -
    - (A) kills, kidnaps, maims, commits an assault resulting in serious bodily injury, or assaults with a dangerous weapon any person within the United States; or
    - (B) creates a substantial risk of serious bodily injury to any other person by destroying or damaging any structure, conveyance, or other real or personal property within the United States or by attempting or conspiring to destroy or damage any structure, conveyance, or other real or personal property within the United States; in violation of the laws of any State, or the United States, shall be punished as prescribed in subsection (c).
  - o (2) Treatment of threats, attempts and conspiracies. - Whoever threatens to commit an offense under paragraph (1), or attempts or conspires to do so, shall be punished under subsection (c).
- (b) Jurisdictional Bases. -
  - o (1) Circumstances. - The circumstances referred to in subsection (a) are -
    - (A) the mail or any facility of interstate or foreign commerce is used in furtherance of the offense;

- (B) the offense obstructs, delays, or affects interstate or foreign commerce, or would have so obstructed, delayed, or affected interstate or foreign commerce if the offense had been consummated;
- (C) the victim, or intended victim, is the United States Government, a member of the uniformed services, or any official, officer, employee, or agent of the legislative, executive, or judicial branches, or of any department or agency, of the United States;
- (D) the structure, conveyance, or other real or personal property is, in whole or in part, owned, possessed, or leased to the United States, or any department or agency of the United States;
- (E) the offense is committed in the territorial sea (including the airspace above and the seabed and subsoil below, and artificial islands and fixed structures erected thereon) of the United States; or
- (F) the offense is committed within the special maritime and territorial jurisdiction of the United States.
  - o (2) Co-conspirators and accessories after the fact. - Jurisdiction shall exist over all principals and co-conspirators of an offense under this section, and accessories after the fact to any offense under this section, if at least one of the circumstances described in subparagraphs (A) through (F) of paragraph (1) is applicable to at least one offender.
- (c) Penalties. -
  - o (1) Penalties. - Whoever violates this section shall be punished -
    - (A) for a killing, or if death results to any person from any other conduct prohibited by this section, by death, or by imprisonment for any term of years or for life;
    - (B) for kidnapping, by imprisonment for any term of years or for life;
    - (C) for maiming, by imprisonment for not more than 35 years;
    - (D) for assault with a dangerous weapon or assault resulting in serious bodily injury, by imprisonment for not more than 30 years;
    - (E) for destroying or damaging any structure, conveyance, or other real or personal property, by imprisonment for not more than 25 years;
    - (F) for attempting or conspiring to commit an offense, for any term of years up to the maximum punishment that would have applied had the offense been completed; and
    - (G) for threatening to commit an offense under this

section, by imprisonment for not more than 10 years.

- o (2) Consecutive sentence. - Notwithstanding any other provision of law, the court shall not place on probation any person convicted of a violation of this section; nor shall the term of imprisonment imposed under this section run concurrently with any other term of imprisonment.
- (d) Proof Requirements. - The following shall apply to prosecutions under this section:
  - o (1) Knowledge. - The prosecution is not required to prove knowledge by any defendant of a jurisdictional base alleged in the indictment.
  - o (2) State law. - In a prosecution under this section that is based upon the adoption of State law, only the elements of the offense under State law, and not any provisions pertaining to criminal procedure or evidence, are adopted.
- (e) Extraterritorial Jurisdiction. - There is extraterritorial Federal jurisdiction -
  - o (1) over any offense under subsection (a), including any threat, attempt, or conspiracy to commit such offense; and (2) over conduct which, under section 3, renders any person an accessory after the fact to an offense under subsection (a).
- (f) Investigative Authority. - In addition to any other investigative authority with respect to violations of this title, the Attorney General shall have primary investigative responsibility for all Federal crimes of terrorism, and the Secretary of the Treasury shall assist the Attorney General at the request of the Attorney General. Nothing in this section shall be construed to interfere with the authority of the United States Secret Service under section 3056.
- (g) Definitions. - As used in this section -
  - o (1) the term "conduct transcending national boundaries" means conduct occurring outside of the United States in addition to the conduct occurring in the United States;
  - o (2) the term "facility of interstate or foreign commerce" has the meaning given that term in section 1958(b)(2);
  - o (3) the term "serious bodily injury" has the meaning given that term in section 1365(g)(3);
  - o (4) the term "territorial sea of the United States" means all waters extending seaward to 12 nautical miles from the baselines of the United States, determined in accordance with international law; and
  - o (5) the term "Federal crime of terrorism" means an offense that -
    - (A) is calculated to influence or affect the conduct of government by intimidation or coercion, or to retaliate against government conduct; and
    - (B) is a violation of -

- (i) section <u>32</u> (relating to destruction of aircraft or aircraft facilities), 37 (relating to violence at international airports), 81 (relating to arson within special maritime and territorial jurisdiction), 175 (relating to biological weapons), 351 (relating to congressional, cabinet, and Supreme Court assassination, kidnapping, and assault), 831 (relating to nuclear materials), 842(m) or (n)(relating to plastic explosives), 844(e) (relating to certain bombings), 844(f) or (i) (relating to arson and bombing of certain property), 930(c), 956 (relating to conspiracy to injure property of a foreign government), 1114 (relating to protection of officers and employees of the United States), 1116 (relating to murder or manslaughter of foreign officials, official guests, or internationally protected persons), 1203 (relating to hostage taking), 1361 (relating to injury of Government property or contracts), 1362 (relating to destruction of communication lines, stations, or systems), 1363 (relating to injury to buildings or property within special maritime and territorial jurisdiction of the United States), 1366 (relating to destruction of an energy facility), 1751 (relating to Presidential and Presidential staff assassination, kidnapping, and assault), 1992, 2152 (relating to injury of fortifications, harbor defenses, or defensive sea areas), 2155 (relating to destruction of national defense materials, premises, or utilities), 2156 (relating to production of defective national defense materials, premises, or utilities), 2280 (relating to violence against maritime navigation), 2281 (relating to violence against maritime fixed platforms), 2332 (relating to certain homicides and other violence against United States nationals occurring outside of the United States), 2332a (relating to use of weapons of mass destruction), 2332b (relating to acts of terrorism transcending national boundaries), 2332c, [1] 2339A (relating to pro-viding material support to terrorists), 2339B (relating to providing material support to terrorist organizations), or 2340A (relating to torture);
- (ii) section <u>236</u> (relating to sabotage of nuclear facilities or fuel) of the Atomic Energy Act of 1954 (42 U.S.C. 2284); or
- (iii) section <u>46502</u> (relating to aircraft piracy) or section <u>60123</u>(b) (relating to destruction of interstate

gas or hazardous liquid pipeline facility) of title 49.

Sec. 2332d. Financial transactions

- (a) Offense. - Except as provided in regulations issued by the Secretary of the Treasury, in consultation with the Secretary of State, whoever, being a United States person, knowing or having reasonable cause to know that a country is designated under section 6(j) of the Export Administration Act (50 U.S.C. App. 2405) as a country supporting international terrorism, engages in a financial transaction with the government of that country, shall be fined under this title, imprisoned for not more than 10 years, or both.
- (b) Definitions. - As used in this section -
    - o (1) the term "financial transaction" has the same meaning as in section 1956(c)(4); and
       (2) the term "United States person" means any -
        - ▪ (A) United States citizen or national;
        - ▪ (B) permanent resident alien;
        - ▪ (C) juridical person organized under the laws of the United States; or
        - ▪ (D) any person in the United States.

Sec. 2339A. Providing material support to terrorists

(a) Offense. - Whoever, within the United States, provides material support or resources or conceals or disguises the nature, location, source, or ownership of material support or resources, knowing or intending that they are to be used in preparation for, or in carrying out, a violation of section 32, 37, 81, 175, 351, 831, 842(m) or (n), 844(f) or (i), 930(c), 956, 1114, 1116, 1203, 1361, 1362, 1363, 1366, 1751, 1992, 2155, 2156, 2280, 2281, 2332, 2332a, 2332b, 2332c, ⟨⟩ or 2340A of this title or section 46502 of title 49, or in preparation for, or in carrying out, the concealment or an escape from the commission of any such violation, shall be fined under this title, imprisoned not more than 10 years, or both.

- (b) Definition. - In this section, the term "material support or resources" means currency or other financial securities, financial services, lodging, training, safehouses, false documentation or identification, communications equipment, facilities, weapons, lethal substances, explosives, personnel, transportation, and other physical assets, except medicine or religious materials.

Sec. 2339B. Providing material support or resources to designated foreign terrorist organizations

- (a) Prohibited Activities. -
    - o (1) Unlawful conduct. - Whoever, within the United States or

subject to the jurisdiction of the United States, knowingly provides material support or resources to a foreign terrorist organization, or attempts or conspires to do so, shall be fined under this title or imprisoned not more than 10 years, or both.

- o (2) Financial institutions. - Except as authorized by the Secretary, any financial institution that becomes aware that it has possession of, or control over, any funds in which a foreign terrorist organization, or its agent, has an interest, shall -
  - § (A) retain possession of, or maintain control over, such funds; and
  (B) report to the Secretary the existence of such funds in accordance with regulations issued by the Secretary.
- (b) Civil Penalty. - Any financial institution that knowingly fails to comply with subsection (a)(2) shall be subject to a civil penalty in an amount that is the greater of -
  - o (A) $50,000 per violation; or
  - o (B) twice the amount of which the financial institution was required under subsection (a)(2) to retain possession or control.
- (c) Injunction. - Whenever it appears to the Secretary or the Attorney General that any person is engaged in, or is about to engage in, any act that constitutes, or would constitute, a violation of this section, the Attorney General may initiate civil action in a district court of the United States to enjoin such violation.
- (d) Extraterritorial Jurisdiction. - There is extraterritorial Federal jurisdiction over an offense under this section.
- (e) Investigations. -
  - o (1) In general. - The Attorney General shall conduct any investigation of a possible violation of this section, or of any license, order, or regulation issued pursuant to this section.
  - o (2) Coordination with the department of the treasury. - The Attorney General shall work in coordination with the Secretary in investigations relating to -
    - ▪ (A) the compliance or noncompliance by a financial institution with the requirements of subsection (a)(2); and
    - • (B) civil penalty proceedings authorized under subsection (b).
  - o (3) Referral. - Any evidence of a criminal violation of this section arising in the course of an investigation by the Secretary or any other Federal agency shall be referred immediately to the Attorney General for further investigation.

    The Attorney General shall timely notify the Secretary of any action taken on referrals from the Secretary, and may refer investigations to the Secretary for remedial licensing or civil penalty action.

- (f) Classified Information in Civil Proceedings Brought by the United States. -
    - o (1) Discovery of classified information by defendants. -
        - (A) Request by united states. - In any civil proceeding under this section, upon request made ex parte and in writing by the United States, a court, upon a sufficient showing, may authorize the United States to -
            - (i) redact specified items of classified information from documents to be introduced into evidence or made available to the defendant through discovery under the Federal Rules of Civil Procedure;
            - (ii) substitute a summary of the information for such classified documents; or
            - (iii) substitute a statement admitting relevant facts that the classified information would tend to prove.
        - (B) Order granting request. - If the court enters an order granting a request under this paragraph, the entire text of the documents to which the request relates shall be sealed and preserved in the records of the court to be made available to the appellate court in the event of an appeal.
        - (C) Denial of request. - If the court enters an order denying a request of the United States under this paragraph, the United States may take an immediate, interlocutory appeal in accordance with paragraph (5). For purposes of such an appeal, the entire text of the documents to which the request relates, together with any transcripts of arguments made ex parte to the court in connection therewith, shall be maintained under seal and delivered to the appellate court.
    - o (2) Introduction of classified information; precautions by court. -
        - (A) Exhibits. - To prevent unnecessary or inadvertent disclosure of classified information in a civil proceeding brought by the United States under this section, the United States may petition the court ex parte to admit, in lieu of classified writings, recordings, or photographs, one or more of the following:
            - (i) Copies of items from which classified information has been redacted.
            - (ii) Stipulations admitting relevant facts that specific classified information would tend to prove.
            - (iii) A declassified summary of the specific classified information.
        - (B) Determination by court. - The court shall grant a

request under this paragraph if the court finds that the redacted item, stipulation, or summary is sufficient to allow the defendant to prepare a defense.

o   (3) Taking of trial testimony. -

- (A) Objection. - During the examination of a witness in any civil proceeding brought by the United States under this subsection, the United States may object to any question or line of inquiry that may require the witness to disclose classified information not previously found to be admissible.

- (B) Action by court. - In determining whether a response is admissible, the court shall take precautions to guard against the compromise of any classified information, including -

  - (i) permitting the United States to provide the court, ex parte, with a proffer of the witness's response to the question or line of inquiry; and

  - (ii) requiring the defendant to provide the court with a proffer of the nature of the information that the defendant seeks to elicit.

- (C) Obligation of defendant. - In any civil proceeding under this section, it shall be the defendant's obligation to establish the relevance and materiality of any classified information sought to be introduced.

o   (4) Appeal. - If the court enters an order denying a request of the United States under this subsection, the United States may take an immediate interlocutory appeal in accordance with paragraph (5).

o   (5) Interlocutory appeal. -

- (A) Subject of appeal. - An interlocutory appeal by the United States shall lie to a court of appeals from a decision or order of a district court -

  - (i) authorizing the disclosure of classified information;

  - (ii) imposing sanctions for nondisclosure of classified information; or

  - (iii) refusing a protective order sought by the United States to prevent the disclosure of classified information.

- (B) Expedited consideration. -

  - (i) In general. - An appeal taken pursuant to this paragraph, either before or during trial, shall be expedited by the court of appeals.

  - (ii) Appeals prior to trial. - If an appeal is of an order made prior to trial, an appeal shall be taken

not later than 10 days after the decision or order appealed from, and the trial shall not commence until the appeal is resolved.
- (iii) Appeals during trial. - If an appeal is taken during trial, the trial court shall adjourn the trial until the appeal is resolved, and the court:
  - (I) shall hear argument on such appeal not later than 4
  days after the adjournment of the trial;
  - (II) may dispense with written briefs other than the
  supporting materials previously submitted to the trial
  court;
  - (III) shall render its decision not later than 4 days
  after argument on appeal; and
  (IV) may dispense with the issuance of a written opinion
  in rendering its decision.
- (C) Effect of ruling. - An interlocutory appeal and decision shall not affect the right of the defendant, in a subsequent appeal from a final judgment, to claim as error reversal by the trial court on remand of a ruling appealed from during trial.

o (6) Construction. - Nothing in this subsection shall prevent the United States from seeking protective orders or asserting privileges ordinarily available to the United States to protect against the disclosure of classified information, including the invocation of the military and State secrets privilege.

- (g) Definitions. - As used in this section -
  o (1) the term "classified information" has the meaning given that term in section 1(a) of the Classified Information Procedures Act (18 U.S.C. App.);
  o (2) the term "financial institution" has the same meaning as in section 5312(a)(2) of title 31, United States Code;
  o (3) the term "funds" includes coin or currency of the United States or any other country, traveler's checks, personal checks, bank checks, money orders, stocks, bonds, debentures, drafts, letters of credit, any other negotiable instrument, and any electronic representation of any of the foregoing;
  o (4) the term "material support or resources" has the same meaning as in section 2339A;
  o (5) the term "Secretary" means the Secretary of the Treasury; and

o (6) the term ''terrorist organization'' means an organization designated as a terrorist organization under section 219 of the Immigration and Nationality Act.

DOCUMENT No. 6

TITLE 22, UNITED STATES CODE, CHAPTER 32 - FOREIGN ASSISTANCE

SUBCHAPTER II - MILITARY ASSISTANCE AND SALES
PART VIII - ANTITERRORISM ASSISTANCE

Sec. 2349aa. General authority

Notwithstanding any other provision of law that restricts assistance to foreign countries (other than sections 2304 and 2371 of this title), the President is authorized to furnish, on such terms and conditions as the President may determine, assistance to foreign countries in order to enhance the ability of their law enforcement personnel to deter terrorists and terrorist groups from engaging in international terrorist acts such as bombing, kidnapping, assassination, hostage taking, and hijacking. Such assistance may include training services and the provision of equipment and other commodities related to bomb detection and disposal, management of hostage situations, physical security, and other matters relating to the detection, deterrence, and prevention of acts of terrorism, the resolution of terrorist incidents, and the apprehension of those involved in such acts.

Sec. 2349aa-1. Purposes

Activities conducted under this part shall be designed -

- (1) to enhance the antiterrorism skills of friendly countries by providing training and equipment to deter and counter terrorism;
- (2) to strengthen the bilateral ties of the United States with friendly governments by offering concrete assistance in this area of great mutual concern; and
- (3) to increase respect for human rights by sharing with foreign civil authorities modern, humane, and effective antiterrorism techniques.

Sec. 2349aa-2. Limitations

- (a) Services and commodities furnished by agency of United States Government; advance payment
  Whenever the President determines it to be consistent with and in furtherance of the purposes of this part, and on such terms and conditions consistent with this chapter as he may determine, any agency of the United States Government is authorized to furnish services and commodi-

ties, without charge to funds available to carry out this part, to an eligible foreign country, subject to payment in advance of the value thereof (within the meaning of section 2403(m) of this title) in United States dollars by the foreign country. Credits and the proceeds of guaranteed loans made available to such countries pursuant to the Arms Export Control Act (22 U.S.C. 2751 et seq.) shall not be used for such payments. Collections under this part shall be credited to the currently applicable appropriation, account, or fund of the agency providing such services and commodities and shall be available for the purposes for which such appropriation, account, or fund is authorized to be used.

- (b) Consultation in development and implementation of assistance
  The Assistant Secretary of State for Democracy, Human Rights, and Labor shall be consulted in the determinations of the foreign countries that will be furnished assistance under this part and determinations of the nature of assistance to be furnished to each such country.
- (c) Arms and ammunition; value of equipment and commodities
  - o   (1) Arms and ammunition may be provided under this part only if they are directly related to antiterrorism assistance.
  - o   (2) The value (in terms of original acquisition cost) of all equipment and commodities provided under this part in any fiscal year shall not exceed 30 percent of the funds made available to carry out this part for that fiscal year.
- (d) Information exchange activities
  This part does not apply to information exchange activities conducted by agencies of the United States Government under other authority for such purposes.

Sec. 2349aa-5. Administrative authorities

Except where expressly provided to the contrary, any reference in any law to subchapter I of this chapter shall be deemed to include reference to this part and any reference in any law to subchapter II of this chapter shall be deemed to exclude reference to this part.

Sec. 2349aa-7. Coordination of all United States terrorism-related assistance to foreign countries

- (a) Responsibility
  The Secretary of State shall be responsible for coordinating all assistance related to international terrorism which is provided by the United States Government to foreign countries.
- (b) Reports
  Not later than February 1 each year, the Secretary of State, in consultation with appropriate United States Government agencies, shall report to the appropriate committees of the Congress on the assistance related to international terrorism which was provided by the United States Govern-

ment during the preceding fiscal year. Such reports may be provided on a classified basis to the extent necessary, and shall specify the amount and nature of the assistance provided.

- (c) Rule of construction
Nothing contained in this section shall be construed to limit or impair the authority or responsibility of any other Federal agency with respect to law enforcement, domestic security operations, or intelligence activities as defined in Executive Order 12333.

Sec. 2349aa-8. Prohibition on imports from and exports to Libya

- (a) Prohibition on imports
Notwithstanding any other provision of law, the President may prohibit any article grown, produced, extracted, or manufactured in Libya from being imported into the United States.
- (b) Prohibition on exports
Notwithstanding any other provision of law, the President may prohibit any goods or technology, including technical data or other information, subject to the jurisdiction of the United States or exported by any person subject to the jurisdiction of the United States, from being exported to Libya.
- (c) "United States" defined
For purposes of this section, the term "United States", when used in a geographical sense, includes territories and possessions of the United States.

Sec. 2349aa-9. Ban on importing goods and services from countries supporting terrorism

- (a) Authority
The President may ban the importation into the United States of any ogood or service from any country which supports terrorism or terrorist organizations or harbors terrorists or terrorist organizations.
- (b) Consultation
The President, in every possible instance, shall consult with the Congress before exercising the authority granted by this section and shall consult regularly with the Congress so long as that authority is being exercised.
- (c) Reports
Whenever the President exercises the authority granted by this section, he shall immediately transmit to the Congress a report specifying -
  - o (1) the country with respect to which the authority is to be exercised and the imports to be prohibited;
  - o (2) the circumstances which necessitate the exercise of such authority;
  - o (3) why the President believes those circumstances justify the exercise of such authority; and
  - o (4) why the President believes the prohibitions are necessary

to deal with those circumstances. At least once during each succeeding 6-month period after transmitting a report pursuant to this subsection, the President shall report to the Congress with respect to the actions taken, since the last such report, pursuant to this section and with respect to any changes which have occurred concerning any information previously furnished pursuant to this subsection.

- (d) "United States" defined
  For purposes of this section, the term "United States" includes territories and possessions of the United States.

Sec. 2349aa-10. Antiterrorism assistance

- (a) Omitted
- (b) Assistance to foreign countries to procure explosives detection devices and other counterterrorism technology
    o (1) Subject to section 2349aa-4(b) of this title, up to $3,000,000 in any fiscal year may be made available -
      (A) to procure explosives detection devices and other counterterrorism technology; and
      (B) for joint counterterrorism research and development projects on such technology conducted with NATO and major non-NATO allies under the auspices of the Technical Support Working Group of the Department of State.
    o (2) As used in this subsection, the term "major non-NATO allies" means those countries designated as major non-NATO allies for purposes of section 2350a(i)(3) of title 10.
- (c) Assistance to foreign countries
  Notwithstanding any other provision of law (except section 2371 of this title) up to $1,000,000 in assistance may be provided to a foreign country for counterterrorism efforts in any fiscal year if -
    o (1) such assistance is provided for the purpose of protecting the property of the United States Government or the life and property of any United States citizen, or furthering the apprehension of any individual involved in any act of terrorism against such property or persons; and
    o (2) the appropriate committees of Congress are notified not later than 15 days prior to the provision of such assistance.

PART I—GENERAL PROVISIONS

Sec. 2377. Prohibition on assistance to countries that aid terrorist states

- (a) Withholding of assistance
  The President shall withhold assistance under this chapter to the government of any country that provides assistance to the government of any

other country for which the Secretary of State has made a determination under section 2371 of this title.

- (b) Waiver
Assistance prohibited by this section may be furnished to a foreign government described in subsection (a) of this section if the President determines that furnishing such assistance is important to the national interests of the United States and, not later than 15 days before obligating such assistance, furnishes a report to the appropriate committees of Congress including -
    - o (1) a statement of the determination;
    - o (2) a detailed explanation of the assistance to be provided;
    - o (3) the estimated dollar amount of the assistance; and
    - o (4) an explanation of how the assistance furthers United States national interests.

Sec. 2378. Prohibition on assistance to countries that provide military equipment to terrorist states

- (a) Prohibition
    - o (1) In general
    The President shall withhold assistance under this chapter to the government of any country that provides lethal military equipment to a country the government of which the Secretary of State has determined is a terrorist government for the purposes of section 2405(j) of title 50, Appendix, or 2371 of this title.
    - o (2) Applicability
    The prohibition under this section with respect to a foreign government shall terminate 1 year after that government ceases to provide lethal military equipment. This section applies with respect to lethal military equipment provided under a contract entered into after April 24, 1996.
- (b) Waiver
Notwithstanding any other provision of law, assistance may be furnished to a foreign government described in subsection (a) of this section if the President determines that furnishing such assistance is important to the national interests of the United States and, not later than 15 days before obligating such assistance, furnishes a report to the appropriate committees of Congress including -
    - o (1) a statement of the determination;
    - o (2) a detailed explanation of the assistance to be provided;
    - o (3) the estimated dollar amount of the assistance; and
    - o (4) an explanation of how the assistance furthers United States national interests.

DOCUMENT No. 7

TITLE 49, UNITED STATES CODE, CHAPTER 449 - SECURITY
SUBCHAPTER I - REQUIREMENTS

Sec. 44901. Screening passengers and property

- (a) General Requirements. - The Administrator of the Federal Aviation Administration shall prescribe regulations requiring screening of all passengers and property that will be carried in a cabin of an aircraft in air transportation or intrastate air transportation. The screening must take place before boarding and be carried out by a weapon-detecting facility or procedure used or operated by an employee or agent of an air carrier, intrastate air carrier, or foreign air carrier.
- (b) Amending Regulations. - Notwithstanding subsection (a) of this section, the Administrator may amend a regulation prescribed under subsection (a) to require screening only to ensure security against criminal violence and aircraft piracy in air transportation and intrastate air transportation.
- (c) Exemptions and Advising Congress on Regulations. - The Administrator -
    o (1) may exempt from this section air transportation operations, except scheduled passenger operations of an air carrier providing air transportation under a certificate issued under section 41102 of this title or a permit issued under section 41302 of this title; and
    o (2) shall advise Congress of a regulation to be prescribed under this section at least 30 days before the effective date of the regulation, unless the Administrator decides an emergency exists requiring the regulation to become effective in fewer than 30 days and notifies Congress of that decision.

Sec. 44902. Refusal to transport passengers and property

- (a) Mandatory Refusal. - The Administrator of the Federal Aviation Administration shall prescribe regulations requiring an air carrier, intrastate air carrier, or foreign air carrier to refuse to transport -
    o (1) a passenger who does not consent to a search under section 44901(a) of this title establishing whether the passenger is carrying unlawfully a dangerous weapon, explosive, or other destructive substance; or
    o (2) property of a passenger who does not consent to a search of the property establishing whether the property unlawfully

contains a dangerous weapon, explosive, or other destructive substance.

- (b) Permissive Refusal. - Subject to regulations of the Administrator, an air carrier, intrastate air carrier, or foreign air carrier may refuse to transport a passenger or property the carrier decides is, or might be, inimical to safety.
- (c) Agreeing to Consent to Search. - An agreement to carry passengers or property in air transportation or intrastate air transportation by an air carrier, intrastate air carrier, or foreign air carrier is deemed to include an agreement that the passenger or property will not be carried if consent to search the passenger or property for a purpose referred to in this section is not given.

Sec. 44903. Air transportation security

- (a) Definition. - In this section, "law enforcement personnel" means individuals -
  - o (1) authorized to carry and use firearms;
  - o (2) vested with the degree of the police power of arrest the Administrator of the Federal Aviation Administration considers necessary to carry out this section; and
  - o (3) identifiable by appropriate indicia of authority.
- (b) Protection Against Violence and Piracy. - The Administrator shall prescribe regulations to protect passengers and property on an aircraft operating in air transportation or intrastate air transportation against an act of criminal violence or aircraft piracy. When prescribing a regulation under this subsection, the Administrator shall -
  - o (1) consult with the Secretary of Transportation, the Attorney General, the heads of other departments, agencies, and instrumentalities of the United States Government, and State and local authorities;
  - o (2) consider whether a proposed regulation is consistent with -
    - (A) protecting passengers; and
    - (B) the public interest in promoting air transportation and intrastate air transportation;
  - o (3) to the maximum extent practicable, require a uniform procedure for searching and detaining passengers and property to ensure -
    - (A) their safety; and
    - (B) courteous and efficient treatment by an air carrier, an agent or employee of an air carrier, and Government, State, and local law enforcement personnel carrying out this section; and
  - o (4) consider the extent to which a proposed regulation will carry out this section.
- (c) Security Programs.
  - o (1) The Administrator shall prescribe regulations under subsec-

tion (b) of this section that require each operator of an airport regularly serving an air carrier holding a certificate issued by the Secretary of Transportation to establish an air transportation security program that provides a law enforcement presence and capability at each of those airports that is adequate to ensure the safety of passengers. The regulations shall authorize the operator to use the services of qualified State, local, and private law enforcement personnel. When the Administrator decides, after being notified by an operator in the form the Administrator prescribes, that not enough qualified State, local, and private law enforcement personnel are available to carry out subsection (b), the Administrator may authorize the operator to use, on a reimbursable basis, personnel employed by the Administrator, or by another department, agency, or instrumentality of the Government with the consent of the head of the department, agency, or instrumentality, to supplement State, local, and private law enforcement personnel. When deciding whether additional personnel are needed, the Administrator shall consider the number of passengers boarded at the airport, the extent of anticipated risk of criminal violence or aircraft piracy at the airport or to the air carrier aircraft operations at the airport, and the availability of qualified State or local law enforcement personnel at the airport.

o (2)

- (A) The Administrator may approve a security program of an airport operator, or an amendment in an existing program, that incorporates a security program of an airport tenant (except an air carrier separately complying with part 108 or 129 of title 14, Code of Federal Regulations) having access to a secured area of the airport, if the program or amendment incorporates -
  - (i) the measures the tenant will use, within the tenant's leased areas or areas designated for the tenant's exclusive use under an agreement with the airport operator, to carry out the security requirements imposed by the Administrator on the airport operator under the access control system requirements of section 107.14 of title 14, Code of Federal Regulations, or under other requirements of part 107 of title 14; and
  - (ii) the methods the airport operator will use to monitor and audit the tenant's compliance with the security requirements and provides that the tenant will be required to pay monetary penalties to the airport operator if the tenant fails to carry out a security requirement under a contractual provision or requirement imposed by the airport operator.
- (B) If the Administrator approves a program or amendment described in subparagraph (A) of this paragraph, the airport

operator may not be found to be in violation of a requirement of this subsection or subsection (b) of this section when the airport operator demonstrates that the tenant or an employee, permittee, or invitee of the tenant is responsible for the violation and that the airport operator has complied with all measures in its security program for securing compliance with its security program by the tenant.

- (d) Authorizing Individuals To Carry Firearms and Make Arrests. - With the approval of the Attorney General and the Secretary of State, the Secretary of Transportation may authorize an individual who carries out air transportation security duties -
  - o (1) to carry firearms; and
  - o (2) to make arrests without warrant for an offense against the United States committed in the presence of the individual or for a felony under the laws of the United States, if the individual reasonably believes the individual to be arrested has committed or is committing a felony.
- (e) Exclusive Responsibility Over Passenger Safety. - The Administrator has the exclusive responsibility to direct law enforcement activity related to the safety of passengers on an aircraft involved in an offense under section 46502 of this title from the moment all external doors of the aircraft are closed following boarding until those doors are opened to allow passengers to leave the aircraft. When requested by the Administrator, other departments, agencies, and instrumentalities of the Government shall provide assistance necessary to carry out this subsection.

Sec. 44904. Domestic air transportation system security

- (a) Assessing Threats. - The Administrator of the Federal Aviation Administration and the Director of the Federal Bureau of Investigation jointly shall assess current and potential threats to the domestic air transportation system. The assessment shall include consideration of the extent to which there are individuals with the capability and intent to carry out terrorist or related unlawful acts against that system and the ways in which those individuals might carry out those acts. The Administrator and the Director jointly shall decide on and carry out the most effective method for continuous analysis and monitoring of security threats to that system.
- (b) Assessing Security. - In coordination with the Director, the Administrator shall carry out periodic threat and vulnerability assessments on security at each airport that is part of the domestic air transportation system. Each assessment shall include consideration of -
  - o (1) the adequacy of security procedures related to the handling and transportation of checked baggage and cargo;
  - o (2) space requirements for security personnel and equipment;
  - o (3) separation of screened and unscreened passengers, baggage, and cargo;

- o (4) separation of the controlled and uncontrolled areas of airport facilities; and
- o (5) coordination of the activities of security personnel of the Administration, the United States Customs Service, the Immigration and Naturalization Service, and air carriers, and of other law enforcement personnel.
- (c) Improving Security. - The Administrator shall take necessary actions to improve domestic air transportation security by correcting any deficiencies in that security discovered in the assessments, analyses, and monitoring carried out under this section.

Sec. 44905. Information about threats to civil aviation

- (a) Providing Information. - Under guidelines the Secretary of Transportation prescribes, an air carrier, airport operator, ticket agent, or individual employed by an air carrier, airport operator, or ticket agent, receiving information (except a communication directed by the United States Government) about a threat to civil aviation shall provide the information promptly to the Secretary.
- (b) Flight Cancellation. - If a decision is made that a particular threat cannot be addressed in a way adequate to ensure, to the extent feasible, the safety of passengers and crew of a particular flight or series of flights, the Administrator of the Federal Aviation Administration shall cancel the flight or series of flights.
- (c) Guidelines on Public Notice.
  - o (1) The President shall develop guidelines for ensuring that public notice is provided in appropriate cases about threats to civil aviation. The guidelines shall identify officials responsible for -
    - (A) deciding, on a case-by-case basis, if public notice of a threat is in the best interest of the United States and the traveling public;
    - (B) ensuring that public notice is provided in a timely and effective way, including the use of a toll-free telephone number; and
    (C) canceling the departure of a flight or series of flights under subsection (b) of this section.
  - o (2) The guidelines shall provide for consideration of -
    - (A) the specificity of the threat;
    - (B) the credibility of intelligence information related to the threat;
    - (C) the ability to counter the threat effectively;
    - (D) the protection of intelligence information sources and methods;
    - (E) cancellation, by an air carrier or the Administrator, of a flight or series of flights instead of public notice;
    - (F) the ability of passengers and crew to take steps to reduce the risk to their safety after receiving public notice of a

threat; and
- (G) other factors the Administrator considers appropriate.
- (d) Guidelines on Notice to Crews. - The Administrator shall develop guidelines for ensuring that notice in appropriate cases of threats to the security of an air carrier flight is provided to the flight crew and cabin crew of that flight.
- (e) Limitation on Notice to Selective Travelers. - Notice of a threat to civil aviation may be provided to selective potential travelers only if the threat applies only to those travelers.
- (f) Restricting Access to Information. - In cooperation with the departments, agencies, and instrumentalities of the Government that collect, receive, and analyze intelligence information related to aviation security, the Administrator shall develop procedures to minimize the number of individuals who have access to information about threats. However, a restriction on access to that information may be imposed only if the restriction does not diminish the ability of the Government to carry out its duties and powers related to aviation security effectively, including providing notice to the public and flight and cabin crews under this section.
- (g) Distribution of Guidelines. - The guidelines developed under this section shall be distributed for use by appropriate officials of the Department of Transportation, the Department of State, the Department of Justice, and air carriers.

Sec. 44906. Foreign air carrier security programs

The Administrator of the Federal Aviation Administration shall continue in effect the requirement of section 129.25 of title 14, Code of Federal Regulations, that a foreign air carrier must adopt and use a security program approved by the Administrator. The Administrator shall not approve a security program of a foreign air carrier under section 129.25, or any successor regulation, unless the security program requires the foreign air carrier in its operations to and from airports in the United States to adhere to the identical security measures that the Administrator requires air carriers serving the same airports to adhere to. The foregoing requirement shall not be interpreted to limit the ability of the Administrator to impose additional security measures on a foreign air carrier or an air carrier when the Administrator determines that a specific threat warrants such additional measures. The Administrator shall prescribe regulations to carry out this section.

Sec. 44907. Security standards at foreign airports

- (a) Assessment.
  - (1) At intervals the Secretary of Transportation considers necessary, the Secretary shall assess the effectiveness of the security measures maintained at -
    - (A) a foreign airport -
      - (i) served by an air carrier;

- - (ii) from which a foreign air carrier serves the United States; or
  - (iii) that poses a high risk of introducing danger to international air travel; and
  - (B) other foreign airports the Secretary considers appropriate.
  - o (2) The Secretary of Transportation shall conduct an assessment under paragraph (1) of this subsection -
    - (A) in consultation with appropriate aeronautic authorities of the government of a foreign country concerned and each air carrier serving the foreign airport for which the Secretary is conducting the assessment;
    - (B) to establish the extent to which a foreign airport effectively maintains and carries out security measures; and
    - (C) by using a standard that will result in an analysis of the security measures at the airport based at least on the standards and appropriate recommended practices contained in Annex 17 to the Convention on International Civil Aviation in effect on the date of the assessment.
  - o (3) Each report to Congress required under section 44938(b) of this title shall contain a summary of the assessments conducted under this subsection.
- (b) Consultation. - In carrying out subsection (a) of this section, the Secretary of Transportation shall consult with the Secretary of State -
  - o (1) on the terrorist threat that exists in each country; and
  - o (2) to establish which foreign airports are not under the de facto control of the government of the foreign country in which they are located and pose a high risk of introducing danger to international air travel.
- (c) Notifying Foreign Authorities. - When the Secretary of Transportation, after conducting an assessment under subsection (a) of this section, decides that an airport does not maintain and carry out effective security measures, the Secretary of Transportation, after advising the Secretary of State, shall notify the appropriate authorities of the government of the foreign country of the decision and recommend the steps necessary to bring the security measures in use at the airport up to the standard used by the Secretary of Transportation in making the assessment.
- (d) Actions When Airports Not Maintaining and Carrying Out Effective Security Measures.
  - o (1) When the Secretary of Transportation decides under this section that an airport does not maintain and carry out effective security measures -
    - (A) the Secretary of Transportation shall -
      - (i) publish the identity of the airport in the Federal Register;
      - (ii) have the identity of the airport posted and displayed prominently at all United States airports at which scheduled

air carrier operations are provided regularly; and
- (iii) notify the news media of the identity of the airport;
- (B) each air carrier and foreign air carrier providing transportation between the United States and the airport shall provide written notice of the decision, on or with the ticket, to each passenger buying a ticket for transportation between the United States and the airport;
- (C) notwithstanding section 40105(b) of this title, the Secretary of Transportation, after consulting with the appropriate aeronautic authorities of the foreign country concerned and each air carrier serving the airport and with the approval of the Secretary of State, may withhold, revoke, or prescribe conditions on the operating authority of an air carrier or foreign air carrier that uses that airport to provide foreign air transportation; and
- (D) the President may prohibit an air carrier or foreign air carrier from providing transportation between the United States and any other foreign airport that is served by aircraft flying to or from the airport with respect to which a decision is made under this section.

o (2)
- (A) Paragraph (1) of this subsection becomes effective -
  - (i) 90 days after the government of a foreign country is notified under subsection (c) of this section if the Secretary of Transportation finds that the government has not brought the
    security measures at the airport up to the standard the Secretary used in making an assessment under subsection (a) of this section; or
  - (ii) immediately on the decision of the Secretary of Transportation under subsection (c) of this section if the Secretary of Transportation decides, after consulting with the Secretary of State, that a condition exists that threatens the
    safety or security of passengers, aircraft, or crew traveling to or from the airport.
  - (B) The Secretary of Transportation immediately shall notify the Secretary of State of a decision under subparagraph (A)(ii) of this paragraph so that the Secretary of State may issue a travel advisory required under section 44908(a) of this title.

o (3) The Secretary of Transportation promptly shall submit to Congress a report (and classified annex if necessary) on action taken under paragraph (1) or (2) of this subsection, including information on attempts made to obtain the cooperation of the government of a foreign country in meeting the standard the Secretary used in assessing the airport under subsection (a) of this section.

o (4) An action required under paragraph (1)(A) and (B) of this subsection is no longer required only if the Secretary of Transportation, in consultation with the Secretary of State, decides that effective security measures are maintained and carried out at the airport. The Secretary of Transportation shall notify Congress when the action is no longer required to be taken.

- (e) Suspensions. - Notwithstanding sections 40105(b) and 40106(b) of this title, the Secretary of Transportation, with the approval of the Secretary of State and without notice or a hearing, shall suspend the right of an air carrier or foreign air carrier to provide foreign air transportation, and the right of a person to operate aircraft in foreign air commerce, to or from a foreign airport when the Secretary of Transportation decides that -
    o (1) a condition exists that threatens the safety or security of passengers, aircraft, or crew traveling to or from that airport; and
    o (2) the public interest requires an immediate suspension of transportation between the United States and that airport.
- (f) Condition of Carrier Authority. - This section is a condition to authority the Secretary of Transportation grants under this part to an air carrier or foreign air carrier.

Sec. 44908. Travel advisory and suspension of foreign assistance

- (a) Travel Advisories. - On being notified by the Secretary of Transportation that the Secretary of Transportation has decided under section 44907(d)(2)(A)(ii) of this title that a condition exists that threatens the safety or security of passengers, aircraft, or crew traveling to or from a foreign airport that the Secretary of Transportation has decided under section 44907 of this title does not maintain and carry out effective security measures, the Secretary of State -
    o (1) immediately shall issue a travel advisory for that airport; and
    o (2) shall publicize the advisory widely.
- (b) Suspending Assistance. - The President shall suspend assistance provided under the Foreign Assistance Act of 1961 (22 U.S.C. 2151 et seq.) or the Arms Export Control Act (22 U.S.C. 2751 et seq.) to a country in which is located an airport with respect to which section 44907(d)(1) of this title becomes effective if the Secretary of State decides the country is a high terrorist threat country. The President may waive this subsection if the President decides, and reports to Congress, that the waiver is required because of national security interests or a humanitarian emergency.
- (c) Actions No Longer Required. - An action required under this section is no longer required only if the Secretary of Transportation has made a decision as provided under section 44907(d)(4) of this title. The Secretary shall notify Congress when the action is no longer required to be taken.

Sec. 44909. Passenger manifests

- (a) Air Carrier Requirements.
  - o (1) Not later than March 16, 1991, the Secretary of Transportation shall require each air carrier to provide a passenger manifest for a flight to an appropriate representative of the Secretary of State -
    - (A) not later than one hour after that carrier is notified of an aviation disaster outside the United States involving that flight; or
    - (B) if it is not technologically feasible or reasonable to comply with clause (A) of this paragraph, then as expeditiously as possible, but not later than 3 hours after the carrier is so notified.
  - o (2) The passenger manifest shall include the following information:
    - (A) the full name of each passenger.
    - (B) the passport number of each passenger, if required for travel.
    - (C) the name and telephone number of a contact for each passenger.
  - o (3) In carrying out this subsection, the Secretary of Transportation shall consider the necessity and feasibility of requiring air carriers to collect passenger manifest information as a condition for passengers boarding a flight of the carrier.
- (b) Foreign Air Carrier Requirements. - The Secretary of Transportation shall consider imposing a requirement on foreign air carriers comparable to that imposed on air carriers under subsection (a)(1) and (2) of this section.

Sec. 44910. Agreements on aircraft sabotage, aircraft hijacking, and airport security

The Secretary of State shall seek multilateral and bilateral agreement on strengthening enforcement measures and standards for compliance related to aircraft sabotage, aircraft hijacking, and airport security.

Sec. 44911. Intelligence

- (a) Definition. - In this section, "intelligence community" means the intelligence and intelligence-related activities of the following units of the United States Government:
  - o (1) the Department of State.
  - o (2) the Department of Defense.
  - o (3) the Department of the Treasury.
  - o (4) the Department of Energy.
  - o (5) the Departments of the Army, Navy, and Air Force.
  - o (6) the Central Intelligence Agency.
  - o (7) the National Security Agency.
  - o (8) the Defense Intelligence Agency.
  - o (9) the Federal Bureau of Investigation.
  - o (10) the Drug Enforcement Administration.
- (b) Policies and Procedures on Report Availability. - The head of each unit

in the intelligence community shall prescribe policies and procedures to ensure that intelligence reports about international terrorism are made available, as appropriate, to the heads of other units in the intelligence community, the Secretary of Transportation, and the Administrator of the Federal Aviation Administration.

- (c) Unit for Strategic Planning on Terrorism. - The heads of the units in the intelligence community shall consider placing greater emphasis on strategic intelligence efforts by establishing a unit for strategic planning on terrorism.
- (d) Designation of Intelligence Officer. - At the request of the Secretary, the Director of Central Intelligence shall designate at least one intelligence officer of the Central Intelligence Agency to serve in a senior position in the Office of the Secretary.
- (e) Written Working Agreements. - The heads of units in the intelligence community, the Secretary, and the Administrator shall review and, as appropriate, revise written working agreements between the intelligence community and the Administrator.

Sec. 44912. Research and development

- (a) Program Requirement. -
  - o (1) The Administrator of the Federal Aviation Administration shall establish and carry out a program to accelerate and expand the research, development, and implementation of technologies and procedures to counteract terrorist acts against civil aviation. The program shall provide for developing and having in place, not later than November 16, 1993, new equipment and procedures necessary to meet the technological challenges presented by terrorism. The program shall include research on, and development of, technological improvements and ways to enhance human performance.
  - o (2) In designing and carrying out the program established under this subsection, the Administrator shall -
    - (A) consult and coordinate activities with other departments, agencies, and instrumentalities of the United States Government doing similar research;
    - (B) identify departments, agencies, and instrumentalities that would benefit from that research; and
    - (C) seek cost-sharing agreements with those departments, agencies, and instrumentalities.
  - o (3) In carrying out the program established under this subsection, the Administrator shall review and consider the annual reports the Secretary of Transportation submits to Congress on transportation security and intelligence.
  - o (4) The Administrator may -
    - (A) make grants to institutions of higher learning and other appropriate research facilities with demonstrated ability to carry out research described in paragraph (1) of this subsection, and fix

the amounts and terms of the grants; and
- o (B) make cooperative agreements with governmental authorities the Administrator decides are appropriate.
- (b) Review of Threats. -
  - o (1) The Administrator shall complete an intensive review of threats to civil aviation, with particular focus on -
    - (A) explosive material that presents the most significant threat to civil aircraft;
    - (B) the minimum amounts, configurations, and types of explosive material that can cause, or would reasonably be expected to cause, catastrophic damage to commercial aircraft in service and expected to be in service in the 10-year period beginning on November 16, 1990;
    - (C) the amounts, configurations, and types of explosive material that can be detected reliably by existing, or reasonably anticipated, near-term explosive detection technologies;
    - (D) the feasibility of using various ways to minimize damage caused by explosive material that cannot be detected reliably by existing, or reasonably anticipated, near-term explosive detection technologies;
    - (E) the ability to screen passengers, carry-on baggage, checked baggage, and cargo; and
    - (F) the technologies that might be used in the future to attempt to destroy or otherwise threaten commercial aircraft and the way in which those technologies can be countered effectively.
  - o (2) The Administrator shall use the results of the review under this subsection to develop the focus and priorities of the program established under subsection (a) of this section.
- (c) Scientific Advisory Panel. - The Administrator shall establish a scientific advisory panel, as a subcommittee of the Research, Engineering and Development Advisory Committee, to review, comment on, advise on the progress of, and recommend modifications in, the program established under subsection (a) of this section, including the need for long-range research programs to detect and prevent catastrophic damage to commercial aircraft by the next generation of terrorist weapons. The panel shall consist of individuals with scientific and technical expertise in -
  - o (1) the development and testing of effective explosive detection systems;
  - o (2) aircraft structure and experimentation to decide on the type and minimum weights of explosives that an effective technology must be capable of detecting;
  - o (3) technologies involved in minimizing airframe damage to aircraft from explosives; and
  - o (4) other scientific and technical areas the Administrator considers appropriate.

Sec. 44913. Explosive detection

- (a) Deployment and Purchase of Equipment.
  - o (1) A deployment or purchase of explosive detection equipment under section 108.7(b)(8) or 108.20 of title 14, Code of Federal Regulations, or similar regulation is required only if the Administrator of the Federal Aviation Administration certifies that the equipment alone, or as part of an integrated system, can detect under realistic air carrier operating conditions the amounts, configurations, and types of explosive material that would likely be used to cause catastrophic damage to commercial aircraft. The Administrator shall base the certification on the results of tests conducted under protocols developed in consultation with expert scientists outside of the Administration. Those tests shall be completed not later than April 16, 1992.
  - o (2) Before completion of the tests described in paragraph (1) of this subsection, but not later than April 16, 1992, the Administrator may require deployment of explosive detection equipment described in paragraph (1) if the Administrator decides that deployment will enhance aviation security significantly. In making that decision, the Administrator shall consider factors such as the ability of the equipment alone, or as part of an integrated system, to detect under realistic air carrier operating conditions the amounts, configurations, and types of explosive material that would likely be used to cause catastrophic damage to commercial aircraft. The Administrator shall notify the Committee on Commerce, Science, and Transportation of the Senate and the Committee on Transportation and Infrastructure of the House of Representatives of a deployment decision made under this paragraph.
  - o (3) Until such time as the Administrator determines that equipment certified under paragraph (1) is commercially available and has successfully completed operational testing as provided in paragraph (1), the Administrator shall facilitate the deployment of such approved commercially available explosive detection devices as the Administrator determines will enhance aviation security significantly. The Administrator shall require that equipment deployed under this paragraph be replaced by equipment certified under paragraph (1) when equipment certified under paragraph (1) becomes commercially available. The Administrator is authorized, based on operational considerations at individual airports, to waive the required installation of commercially available equipment under paragraph (1) in the interests of aviation security. The Administrator may permit the requirements of this paragraph to be met at airports by the deployment of dogs or other appropriate animals to supplement equipment

for screening passengers, baggage, mail, or cargo for explosives or weapons.

o (4) This subsection does not prohibit the Administrator from purchasing or deploying explosive detection equipment described in paragraph (1) of this subsection.

• (b) Grants. - The Secretary of Transportation may provide grants to continue the Explosive Detection K-9 Team Training Program to detect explosives at airports and on aircraft.

Sec. 44914. Airport construction guidelines

In consultation with air carriers, airport authorities, and others the Administrator of the Federal Aviation Administration considers appropriate, the Administrator shall develop guidelines for airport design and construction to allow for maximum security enhancement. In developing the guidelines, the Administrator shall consider the results of the assessment carried out under section 44904(a) of this title.

Sec. 44915. Exemptions

The Administrator of the Federal Aviation Administration may exempt from sections 44901, 44903(a)-(c) and (e), 44906, 44935, and 44936 of this title airports in Alaska served only by air carriers that -

o (1) hold certificates issued under section 41102 of this title;

o (2) operate aircraft with certificates for a maximum gross takeoff weight of less than 12,500 pounds; and

o (3) board passengers, or load property intended to be carried in an aircraft cabin, that will be screened under section 44901 of this title at another airport in Alaska before the passengers board, or the property is loaded on, an aircraft for a place outside Alaska.

Sec. 44916. Assessments and evaluations

• (a) Periodic Assessments. - The Administrator shall require each air carrier and airport (including the airport owner or operator in cooperation with the air carriers and vendors serving each airport) that provides for intrastate, interstate, or foreign air transportation to conduct periodic vulnerability assessments of the security systems of that air carrier or airport, respectively. The Administration shall perform periodic audits of such assessments.

• (b) Investigations. - The Administrator shall conduct periodic and unannounced inspections of security systems of airports and air carriers to determine the effectiveness and vulnerabilities of such systems. To the extent allowable by law, the Administrator may provide for anonymous tests of those security systems.

DOCUMENT No. 8

UNITED STATES v. YUNIS
924 F.2d 1086
C.A.D.C.,1991.
Decided Jan. 29, 1991.

*1088 **131 Appeal from the United States District Court for the District of Columbia (Criminal No. 87-00377).

Opinion for the Court filed by Chief Judge MIKVA.

MIKVA, Chief Judge:
Appellant Fawaz Yunis challenges his convictions on conspiracy, aircraft piracy, and hostage-taking charges stemming from the hijacking of a Jordanian passenger aircraft *1089 **132 in Beirut, Lebanon. He appeals from orders of the district court denying his pretrial motions relating to jurisdiction, illegal arrest, alleged violations of the Posse Comitatus Act, and the government's withholding of classified documents during discovery. Yunis also challenges the district court's jury instructions as erroneous and prejudicial.

Although this appeal raises novel issues of domestic and international law, we reject Yunis' objections and affirm the convictions.

I. BACKGROUND

On June 11, 1985, appellant and four other men boarded Royal Jordanian Airlines Flight 402 ("Flight 402") shortly before its scheduled departure from Beirut, Lebanon. They wore civilian clothes and carried military assault rifles, ammunition bandoleers, and hand grenades. Appellant took control of the cockpit and forced the pilot to take off immediately. The remaining hijackers tied up Jordanian air marshals assigned to the flight and held the civilian passengers, including two American citizens, captive in their seats. The hijackers explained to the crew and passengers that they wanted the plane to fly to Tunis, where a conference of the Arab League was under way. The hijackers further explained that they wanted a meeting with delegates to the conference and that their ultimate goal was removal of all Palestinians from Lebanon.

After a refueling stop in Cyprus, the airplane headed for Tunis but turned away when authorities blocked the airport runway. Following a refueling stop at Palermo, Sicily, another attempt to land in Tunis, and a second stop in Cyprus, the plane returned to Beirut, where more hijackers came aboard. These reinforcements included an official of Lebanon's Amal Militia, the group at whose direction Yunis claims he acted. The plane then took off for Syria, but was turned away and went back to Beirut. There, the hijackers released the passengers, held a press conference reiterating their demand that Palestinians leave Lebanon, blew up the plane, and fled from the airport.

An American investigation identified Yunis as the probable leader of the hijackers and prompted U.S. civilian and military agencies, led by the Federal Bureau of Investigation (FBI), to plan Yunis' arrest. After obtaining an arrest warrant, the FBI put "Operation Goldenrod" into effect in September 1987. Undercover FBI agents lured Yunis onto a yacht in the eastern Mediterranean Sea with promises of a drug deal, and arrested him once the vessel entered international waters. The agents transferred Yunis to a United States Navy munitions ship and interrogated him for several days as the vessel steamed toward a second rendezvous, this time with a Navy aircraft carrier. Yunis was flown to Andrews Air Force Base from the aircraft carrier, and taken from there to Washington, D.C. In Washington, Yunis was arraigned on an original indictment charging him with conspiracy, hostage taking, and aircraft damage. A grand jury subsequently returned a superseding indictment adding additional aircraft damage counts and a charge of air piracy.

Yunis filed several pretrial motions, among them a motion to suppress statements he made while aboard the munitions ship. In *United States v. Yunis (Yunis I),* 859 F.2d 953 (D.C.Cir.1988), this court reversed a district court order suppressing the statements, and authorized their introduction at trial. We revisited the case on a second interlocutory appeal relating to discovery of classified information, reversing the district court's disclosure order. *United States v. Yunis (Yunis II),* 867 F.2d 617 (D.C.Cir.1989).

Yunis admitted participation in the hijacking at trial but denied parts of the government's account and offered the affirmative defense of obedience to military orders, asserting that he acted on instructions given by his superiors in Lebanon's Amal Militia. The jury convicted Yunis of conspiracy, 18 U.S.C. § 371 (1988), hostage taking, 18 U.S.C. § 1203 (1988), and air piracy, 49 U.S.C. App. § 1472(n) (1988). However, it acquitted him of three other *1090 **133 charged offenses that went to trial: violence against people on board an aircraft, 18 U.S.C. § 32(b)(1) (1988), aircraft damage, 18 U.S.C. § 32(b)(2) (1988), and placing a destructive device aboard an aircraft, 18 U.S.C. § 32(b)(3) (1988). The district court imposed concurrent sentences of five years for conspiracy, thirty years for hostage taking, and twenty years for air piracy. Yunis appeals his conviction and seeks dismissal of the indictment.

II. ANALYSIS

Yunis argues that the district court lacked subject matter and personal jurisdiction to try him on the charges of which he was convicted, that the indictment should have been dismissed because the government seized him in violation of the Posse Comitatus Act and withheld classified materials useful to his defense, and that the convictions should be reversed because of errors in the jury instructions. We consider these claims in turn.

A. *Jurisdictional Claims*

Yunis appeals first of all from the district court's denial of his motion to dismiss for lack of subject matter and personal jurisdiction. *See United States v. Yunis,* 681

F.Supp. 896 (D.D.C.1988). Appellant's principal claim is that, as a matter of domestic law, the federal hostage taking and air piracy statutes do not authorize assertion of federal jurisdiction over him. Yunis also suggests that a contrary construction of these statutes would conflict with established principles of international law, and so should be avoided by this court. Finally, appellant claims that the district court lacked personal jurisdiction because he was seized in violation of American law.

1. Hostage Taking Act

The Hostage Taking Act provides, in relevant part:

(a) [W]hoever, whether inside or outside the United States, seizes or detains and threatens to kill, to injure, or to continue to detain another person in order to compel a third person or a governmental organization to do or to abstain from any act ... shall be punished by imprisonment by any term of years or for life. (b)(1) It is not an offense under this section if the conduct required for the offense occurred outside the United States unless—

(A) the offender or the person seized or detained is a national of the United States;

(B) the offender is found in the United States; or

(C) the governmental organization sought to be compelled is the Government of the United States.

18 U.S.C. § 1203. Yunis claims that this statute cannot apply to an individual who is brought to the United States by force, since those convicted under it must be "found in the United States." But this ignores the law's plain language. Subsections (A), (B), and (C) of section 1203(b)(1) offer *independent* bases for jurisdiction where "the offense occurred outside the United States." Since two of the passengers on Flight 402 were U.S. citizens, section 1203(b)(1)(A), authorizing assertion of U.S. jurisdiction where "the offender or the person seized or detained is a national of the United States," is satisfied. The statute's jurisdictional requirement has been met regardless of whether or not Yunis was "found" within the United States under section 1203(b)(1)(B).

Appellant's argument that we should read the Hostage Taking Act differently to avoid tension with international law falls flat. Yunis points to no treaty obligations of the United States that give us pause. Indeed, Congress intended through the Hostage Taking Act to execute the International Convention Against the Taking of Hostages, which authorizes any signatory state to exercise jurisdiction over persons who take its nationals hostage "if that State considers it appropriate." International Convention Against the Taking of Hostages, *opened for signature* Dec. 18, 1979, art. 5, para. 1, 34 U.N. GAOR Supp. (No. 39), 18 I.L.M. 1456, 1458. See H.R. CONF. REP. No. 1159, 98th Cong., 2d Sess. *1091 **134 418 (1984), *reprinted in* 1984 U.S.CODE CONG. & ADMIN.NEWS 3182, 3710, 3714.

Nor is jurisdiction precluded by norms of customary international law. The district court concluded that two jurisdictional theories of international law, the "universal principle" and the "passive personal principle," supported assertion of U.S. jurisdiction to prosecute Yunis on hijacking and hostage-taking charges. *See Yunis, 681 F.Supp. at 899-903.* Under the universal principle, states may prescribe and prosecute "certain offenses recognized by the community of nations as of universal concern, such as piracy, slave trade, attacks on or hijacking of aircraft,

genocide, war crimes, and perhaps certain acts of terrorism," even absent any
special connection between the state and the offense. *See* Restatement (Third) of
the Foreign Relations Law of the United States §§ 404, 423 (1987) [hereinafter
Restatement]. Under the passive personal principle, a state may punish non-
nationals for crimes committed against its nationals outside of its territory, at least
where the state has a particularly strong interest in the crime. *See id.* at § 402
comment g; *United States v. Benitez, 741 F.2d 1312, 1316 (11th Cir.1984)* (passive
personal principle invoked to approve prosecution of Colombian citizen convicted
of shooting U.S. drug agents in Colombia), *cert. denied*, 471 U.S. 1137, 105 S.Ct.
2679, 86 L.Ed.2d 698 (1985).
Relying primarily on the RESTATEMENT, Yunis argues that hostage taking has
not been recognized as a universal crime and that the passive personal principle
authorizes assertion of jurisdiction over alleged hostage takers only where the
victims were seized because they were nationals of the prosecuting state. Whatever
merit appellant's claims may have as a matter of international law, they cannot
prevail before this court. Yunis seeks to portray international law as a self-executing
code that trumps domestic law whenever the two conflict. That effort miscon-
ceives the role of judges as appliers of international law and as participants in the
federal system. Our duty is to enforce the Constitution, laws, and treaties of the
United States, not to conform the law of the land to norms of customary international law. *See* U.S. CONST. art. VI. As we said in *Committee of U.S. Citizens
Living in Nicaragua v. Reagan, 859 F.2d 929 (D.C.Cir.1988)*: "Statutes inconsistent
with principles of customary international law may well lead to international law
violations. But within the domestic legal realm, that inconsistent statute simply
modifies or supersedes customary international law to the extent of the inconsis-
tency." *Id.* at 938. *See also Federal Trade Comm'n v. Compagnie de Saint-Gobain-Pont-
a-Mousson, 636 F.2d 1300, 1323 (D.C.Cir.1980)* (U.S. courts "obligated to give effect
to an unambiguous exercise by Congress of its jurisdiction to prescribe even if such
an exercise would exceed the limitations imposed by international law").
To be sure, courts should hesitate to give penal statutes extraterritorial effect
absent a clear congressional directive. *See Foley Bros. v. Filardo, 336 U.S. 281, 285, 69
S.Ct. 575, 577, 93 L.Ed. 680 (1949); United States v. Bowman, 260 U.S. 94, 98, 43
S.Ct. 39, 41, 67 L.Ed. 149 (1922)*. Similarly, courts will not blind themselves to
potential violations of international law where legislative intent is ambiguous. *See
Murray v. The Schooner Charming Betsy, 6 U.S. (2 Cranch) 64, 118, 2 L.Ed. 208
(1804)* ("[A]n act of congress ought never to be construed to violate the law of
nations, if any other possible construction remains...."). But the statute in question
reflects an unmistakable congressional intent, consistent with treaty obligations of
the United States, to authorize prosecution of those who take Americans hostage
abroad no matter where the offense occurs or where the offender is found. Our
inquiry can go no further.
2. Antihijacking Act
    The Antihijacking Act provides for criminal punishment of persons who hijack
aircraft operating wholly outside the "special aircraft jurisdiction" of the United
States, provided that the hijacker is later "found in the United States." 49 U.S.C.
*1092 **135 App. § 1472(n). Flight 402, a Jordanian aircraft operating outside of

the United States, was not within this nation's special aircraft jurisdiction. *See* 49 U.S.C. App. § 1301. Yunis urges this court to interpret the statutory requirement that persons prosecuted for air piracy must be "found" in the United States as precluding prosecution of alleged hijackers who are brought here to stand trial. But the issue before us is more fact-specific, since Yunis was indicted for air piracy while awaiting trial on hostage-taking and other charges; we must determine whether, once arrested and brought to this country on those other charges, Yunis was subject to prosecution under the Antihijacking Act as well.

The Antihijacking Act of 1974 was enacted to fulfill this nation's responsibilities under the Convention for the Suppression of Unlawful Seizure of Aircraft (the "Hague Convention"), which requires signatory nations to extradite or punish hijackers "present in" their territory. Convention for the Suppression of Unlawful Seizure of Aircraft, Dec. 16, 1970, art. 4, para. 2, Dec. 16, 1970, 22 U.S.T. 1643, 1645, T.I.A.S. No. 7192. *See* H. REP. No. 885, 93d Cong., 2d Sess. 10 (1974), *reprinted in* 1974 U.S.Code Cong. & Admin.News 3975, 3978; S. REP. No. 13, 93d Cong., 1st Sess. 1, 3 (1973). This suggests that Congress intended the statutory term "found in the United States" to parallel the Hague Convention's "present in [a contracting state's] territory," a phrase which does not indicate the voluntariness limitation urged by Yunis. Moreover, Congress interpreted the Hague Convention as requiring the United States to extradite or prosecute "offenders in its custody," evidencing no concern as to how alleged hijackers came within U.S. territory. S. REP. No. 13, 93d Cong., 1st Sess. at 3; *see* H. REP. No. 885, 93d Cong., 2d Sess. at 10, 1974 U.S.Code Cong. & Admin.News 3978 (Hague Convention designed to close "gap" in Tokyo Convention, which did not require states to prosecute or extradite hijackers "in [their] custody"). From this legislative history we conclude that Yunis was properly indicted under section 1472(n) once in the United States and under arrest on other charges.

The district court correctly found that international law does not restrict this statutory jurisdiction to try Yunis on charges of air piracy. *See Yunis*, 681 F.Supp. at 899-903. Aircraft hijacking may well be one of the few crimes so clearly condemned under the law of nations that states may assert universal jurisdiction to bring offenders to justice, even when the state has no territorial connection to the hijacking and its citizens are not involved. *See id.* at 900-01; *United States v. Georgescu*, 723 F.Supp. 912, 919 (E.D.N.Y.1989); RESTATEMENT § 404 & reporters' note 1, § 423; Randall, *Universal Jurisdiction under International Law*, 66 TEX.L.REV. 785, 815-34 (1988). But in any event we are satisfied that the Antihijacking Act authorizes assertion of federal jurisdiction to try Yunis regardless of hijacking's status vel non as a universal crime. Thus, we affirm the district court on this issue.

3. Legality of Seizure

Yunis further argues that even if the district court had jurisdiction to try him, it should have declined to exercise that jurisdiction in light of the government's allegedly outrageous conduct in bringing him to the United States. This claim was rejected by the district court before trial. *See United States v. Yunis*, 681 F.Supp. 909, 918-21 (D.D.C.1988), *rev'd on other grounds*, 859 F.2d 953 (*Yunis I*).

Principally, Yunis relies on *United States v. Toscanino*, 500 F.2d 267 (2d Cir.1974), in which the court held that due process requires courts to divest themselves of personal jurisdiction acquired through "the government's deliberate, unnecessary and unreasonable invasion of the accused's constitutional rights." *Id.* at 275. *Toscanino* establishes, at best, only a very limited exception to the general rule (known as the *"Ker- Frisbie* doctrine") that "the power of a court to try a person for crime is not impaired by the fact that he had been brought within the court's jurisdiction by reason of a 'forcible abduction.' " *Frisbie v. Collins,* 342 U.S. 519, 522, 72 S.Ct. 509, 511, 96 L.Ed. 541 (1952) (citing, *inter alia, Ker v. Illinois,* 119 U.S. 436, 7 *1093 **136 S.Ct. 225, 30 L.Ed. 421 (1886)). *Toscanino's* rule has, moreover, been limited to cases of "torture, brutality, and similar outrageous conduct," *United States* ex rel. *Lujan v. Gengler,* 510 F.2d 62, 65 (2d Cir.), *cert. denied,* 421 U.S. 1001, 95 S.Ct. 2400, 44 L.Ed.2d 668 (1975), and the Supreme Court has since reaffirmed the *Ker-Frisbie* doctrine, *see Immigration and Naturalization Serv. v. Lopez-Mendoza,* 468 U.S. 1032, 1039, 104 S.Ct. 3479, 3483, 82 L.Ed.2d 778 (1984); *United States v. Crews,* 445 U.S. 463, 474, 100 S.Ct. 1244, 1251, 63 L.Ed.2d 537 (1980).

Even assuming, arguendo, that a district court could correctly dismiss a case otherwise properly before it for the reasons given in *Toscanino,* we find no merit in Yunis' claim. In *Yunis I,* we reviewed the facts of Operation Goldenrod in some detail, including the deception used to arrest Yunis, his injuries and hardships while in custody, and the delay between his arrest and arraignment in the United States. The court sought to determine whether or not these circumstances voided Yunis' waiver of Fifth and Sixth Amendment rights; we concluded that while the government's conduct was neither "picture perfect" nor "a model for law enforcement behavior," the "discomfort and surprise" to which appellant was subjected did not render his waiver invalid. *Yunis I,* 859 F.2d at 969. Similarly, we now find nothing in the record suggesting the sort of intentional, outrageous government conduct necessary to sustain appellant's jurisdictional argument. *Cf. Sami v. United States,* 617 F.2d 755, 774 (D.C.Cir.1979) (finding "no shocking behavior characterized by abduction or brutality which would support an actionable constitutional claim").

B. *Posse Comitatus Act*

Next, Yunis appeals from the district court's denial of his motion to dismiss on the basis of the government's alleged violation of the Posse Comitatus Act, 18 U.S.C. § 1385 (1988), which establishes criminal penalties for willful use of "any part of the Army or the Air Force" in law enforcement, unless expressly authorized by law. *See United States v. Yunis,* 681 F.Supp. 891 (D.D.C.1988). Despite the Posse Comitatus Act's express limitation to the Army and Air Force, appellant seeks dismissal of the indictment on the grounds that the Navy played a direct role in Operation Goldenrod.

We cannot agree that Congress' words admit of any ambiguity. By its terms, 18 U.S.C. § 1385 places no restrictions on naval participation in law enforcement operations; an earlier version of the measure would have expressly extended the bill to the Navy, but the final legislation was attached to an Army appropriations bill and its language was accordingly limited to that service. *See* H.R. REP. No. 71, Part II, 97th Cong., 1st Sess. 4 (1981), *reprinted in* 1981 U.S.Code Cong. &

Admin.News 1781, 1786 [hereinafter H.R. REP. No. 71]; Note, *The* Posse Comitatus *Act: Reconstruction Politics Reconsidered,* 13 AM.CRIM.L.REV. 703, 709-10 (1976). Reference to the Air Force was added in 1956, consistent with reassignment of Army aviation responsibilities to that new branch of the military. *See* H.R. REP. No. 71 at 4, 1981 U.S.Code Cong. & Admin.News 1786. Nothing in this history suggests that we should defy the express language of the Posse Comitatus Act by extending it to the Navy, and we decline to do so. *Accord United States v. Roberts,* 779 F.2d 565, 567 (9th Cir.), *cert. denied,* 479 U.S. 839, 107 S.Ct. 142, 93 L.Ed.2d 84 (1986); *see* H.R. REP. No. 71 at 4, U.S.Code Cong. & Admin.News 1786 (Navy "not legally bound" by Posse Comitatus Act).

Furthermore, some courts have taken the view that the Posse Comitatus Act imposes no restriction on use of American armed forces abroad, noting that Congress intended to preclude military intervention in domestic civil affairs. *See Chandler v. United States,* 171 F.2d 921, 936 (1st Cir.1948), *cert. denied,* 336 U.S. 918, 69 S.Ct. 640, 93 L.Ed. 1081 (1949); *D'Aquino v. United States,* 192 F.2d 338, 351 (9th Cir.1951), *cert. denied,* 343 U.S. 935, 72 S.Ct. 772, 96 L.Ed. 1343 (1952). And even if these difficulties could be overcome, a remedial problem would remain, as dismissal of all charges against Yunis might well be *1094 **137 an inappropriate remedy if violations of the Posse Comitatus Act were found. *See United States v. Cotten,* 471 F.2d 744, 749 (9th Cir.) (rejecting dismissal as remedy for alleged violation of Posse Comitatus Act on *Ker-Frisbie* grounds), *cert. denied,* 411 U.S. 936, 93 S.Ct. 1913, 36 L.Ed.2d 396 (1973); *see also United States v. Hartley,* 796 F.2d 112, 115 (5th Cir.1986) (noting courts' hesitation to adopt exclusionary rule for violations of Posse Comitatus Act); *United States v. Roberts,* 779 F.2d at 568 (refusing to adopt exclusionary rule).

Nor is Yunis helped by 10 U.S.C. § 375 (1988), which requires the Secretary of Defense to issue regulations prohibiting "direct participation" by military personnel in a civilian "search, seizure, arrest, or other similar activity" unless expressly authorized by law. Reliance on this provision faces the same remedial hurdle as direct reliance on the Posse Comitatus Act: Under the *Ker-Frisbie* doctrine, outright dismissal of the charges against Yunis would not be an appropriate remedy for legal violations relating to his arrest. *See United States v. Crews,* 445 U.S. at 474, 100 S.Ct. at 1251. Nor would a violation of the regulations at issue amount to a constitutional violation, making application of an exclusionary rule or similar prophylactic measures inappropriate. *See United States v. Caceres,* 440 U.S. 741, 754-55, 99 S.Ct. 1465, 1472-73, 59 L.Ed.2d 733 (1979).

In any event, we agree with the district court that no governmental illegality occurred. Regulations issued under 10 U.S.C. § 375 require Navy compliance with the restrictions of the Posse Comitatus Act, but interpret that Act as allowing "indirect assistance" to civilian authorities that does not "subject civilians to the exercise of military power that is regulatory, proscriptive, or compulsory in nature." 32 C.F.R. § 213.10(a)(7) (1987). The regulations are consistent with judicial interpretations of the Posse Comitatus Act; in fact, they incorporate one of three tests employed to identify violations. *See Yunis,* 681 F.Supp. at 892 (setting out three tests); *United States v. McArthur,* 419 F.Supp. 186, 194 (D.N.D.1975) ("[T]he feared use which is prohibited by the posse comitatus statute is that which is regulatory, proscriptive or compulsory in nature ...."), *aff'd sub nom. United States v. Casper,* 541 F.2d 1275 (8th Cir.1976), *cert. denied,* 430 U.S. 970, 97 S.Ct. 1654, 52 L.Ed.2d 362 (1977).

The district court found that Navy personnel played only a "passive" role in housing, transporting, and caring for Yunis while he was in the custody of the FBI, and that "[n]one of the Navy's activities constituted the exercise of regulatory, proscriptive, or compulsory military power." *Yunis,* 681 F.Supp. at 895-96. Nor did the Navy's participation in Operation Goldenrod violate either of the other judicial tests for violations of the Posse Comitatus Act: The Navy's role did not amount to "direct active involvement in the execution of the laws," and it did not "pervade the activities of civilian authorities." *Id.* at 895. We see no error in this assessment of the record, and accordingly conclude that no violation of military regulations occurred.

C. *Discovery Claim*

Yunis appeals from the district court's denial of his motion to dismiss on the basis that pre-trial discovery provisions of the Classified Information Procedures Act (CIPA), 18 U.S.C. App. (1988), infringe upon procedural protections guaranteed him by the Fifth and Sixth Amendments. *See* Pretrial Memorandum Order No. 13, *Yunis,* Crim. No. 87-0377 (D.D.C. Feb. 15, 1989), *reproduced in* Appellant's Appendix at Tab 14. In light of our holding in *Yunis II* that CIPA "creates no new rights of or limits on discovery" of classified material, but only requires courts to consider secrecy concerns when applying general discovery rules, we find no merit in this claim. *Yunis II,* 867 F.2d at 621-22; *accord United States v. Anderson,* 872 F.2d 1508, 1514 (11th Cir.) ("[N]o new substantive law was created by the enactment of CIPA."), *cert. denied,* 493 U.S. 1004, 110 S.Ct. 566, 107 L.Ed.2d 560 (1989); *cf. United States v. Pringle,* 751 F.2d 419, 427-28 (1st Cir.1984) (rejecting due process challenge to protection of classified information against discovery).

*1095 **138 Yunis also objects to the district court's refusal to order the government to produce records of conversations between Flight 402 and the Beirut control tower. After *ex parte, in camera* review of classified materials relevant to Yunis' various discovery requests, the trial court ordered disclosure of numerous documents, including "[a]ll audio or video tapes and/or transcripts of conversations between defendant and all airport authorities covering the period of the alleged hijacking...." Order, *Yunis,* Crim. No. 87-0377 (D.D.C. July 18, 1988), *reproduced in* Appellant's Appendix at Tab 7. Upon the government's motion for reconsideration, however, the court narrowed this disclosure order by excluding materials, including tapes and transcripts of conversations with airport authorities, that "do not help the defendant's cause." Pretrial Memorandum Order No. 6, *Yunis,* Crim. No. 87- 0377, 1988 WL 16302 (Sept. 27, 1988), *reproduced in* Appellant's Appendix at Tab 9. Yunis subsequently renewed his request for conversations between Yunis and the Beirut tower, claiming that these transcripts were "vital to understand what outside influence or 'orders' were being transmitted to the hijackers by person(s) not on the plane." *See* Defendant's Reply to Government's Opposition to Defendant's Sixth Motion to Compel Discovery at 5 (filed Feb. 22, 1989), *reproduced in* Appellant's Appendix at Tab 13. Relying on its earlier rulings, the district court denied the request. Pretrial Memorandum Order

No. 16, *Yunis*, Crim. No. 87-0377 (Feb. 27, 1989), *reproduced in* Appellant's Appendix at Tab 15. Yunis now appeals from that denial.

To prevail on a discovery request for classified information, a defendant must make a threshold showing that the requested material is relevant to his case. *Yunis II,* 867 F.2d at 623. If this "low hurdle" is successfully jumped, the court must determine whether or not the government has asserted a "colorable" claim to privilege. If the government has asserted such a claim, the defendant must show that the information would be helpful to his defense. *Id.* We never have had occasion to adopt a rule to guide trial courts when all these showings are made, and we do not do so here; other circuits, however, have endorsed a balancing approach. *See United States v. Sarkissian,* 841 F.2d 959, 965 (9th Cir.1988); *United States v. Smith,* 780 F.2d 1102, 1110 (4th Cir.1985).

Having ourselves reviewed *in camera* the government's classified submissions to the district court, we find very little in them that is both responsive to the discovery request at issue and relevant in any way to Yunis' trial. We certainly agree with the court below that they reveal no information within the scope of Yunis' discovery request that would have helped him at trial. Moreover, *Yunis II* establishes that the government has at least a colorable interest in avoiding release of information that might reveal "the time, place, and nature of the government's ability to intercept the conversations at all." *Yunis II,* 867 F.2d at 623. Under these circumstances, the district court properly declined to order the government to release classified information responsive to Yunis' discovery request.

D. *Jury Instructions*

Lastly, Yunis challenges the district court's instructions to the jury insofar as they relate to intent requirements of the federal hostage taking, hijacking, and conspiracy statutes and to appellant's affirmative defense of obedience to military orders. In so doing, appellant does not come before an "impregnable citadel[ ] of technicality." *United States v. Hasting,* 461 U.S. 499, 509, 103 S.Ct. 1974, 1980, 76 L.Ed.2d 96 (1983) (quoting R. TRAYNOR, THE RIDDLE OF HARMLESS ERROR 14 (1970) (citation omitted)). Trial courts, not the courts of appeals, are the principal bulwarks against injustice in our judicial system, and their resolution of the myriad questions that arise in the course of a criminal trial must be afforded deference. As the Supreme Court has "stressed on more than one occasion, the Constitution entitles a criminal defendant to a fair trial, not a perfect one." *Delaware v. Van Arsdall,* 475 U.S. 673, 681, 106 S.Ct. 1431, 1436, 89 *1096 **139 L.Ed.2d 674 (1986) (citations omitted). In particular, appellate judges ought not substitute their prejudices regarding jury instructions or their notions of apt phraseology for the experience of trial judges in such matters; our more limited responsibility is to ensure that the law is correctly stated for jurors to apply. Where the indispensable prerequisites for a fair trial have been afforded, we will not overturn a conviction just because an awkward word was used in instructing the jury, or even because we would have sustained a defense objection that was overruled. Instead, we look at the *entire record* of the proceedings below and ignore errors that do not undermine confidence in the conviction when viewed in light of all that took place. *See Rose v. Clark,* 478 U.S. 570, 576-79, 106 S.Ct. 3101, 3105-07, 92 L.Ed.2d 460 (1986); *Hasting,* 461 U.S. at 507-09, 103 S.Ct. at 1979-81; *Chapman*

v. California, 386 U.S. 18, 21-24, 87 S.Ct. 824, 826-28, 17 L.Ed.2d 705 (1967);
Kotteakos v. United States, 328 U.S. 750, 762-65, 66 S.Ct. 1239, 1246-48, 90 L.Ed.
1557 (1946). With these precepts in mind, we now turn to appellant's specific
allegations of error in the instructions given by the trial judge.
1. Intent Requirements
Yunis claims that the Antihijacking Act, 49 U.S.C.App. § 1472(n), and the Hostage
Taking Act, 18 U.S.C. § 1203, make specific intent an element of the offenses they
establish, and that the district court erred in failing to adopt jury instructions
offered by the defense that would have made this clear. In appellant's view, the trial
judge's instruction that Yunis could be convicted on these counts only if he acted
"intentionally, deliberately and knowingly" was inadequate. Transcript of Jury
Instructions, March 10, 1989, at 17-18, 20 [hereinafter "Instructions"].

49 U.S.C. App. § 1472(n) suggests no specific intent requirement on its face,
criminalizing any "unlawful" hijacking of an aircraft. Nor do judicial interpretations of related statutes support appellant's position. In fact, courts have interpreted a companion provision criminalizing domestic hijacking, 49 U.S.C. App. §
1472(i), as requiring only general criminal intent, even though (unlike section
1472(n)) it specifies that hijackers must act with "wrongful intent." _See United
States v. Castaneda-Reyes,_ 703 F.2d 522, 525 (11th Cir.), _cert. denied,_ 464 U.S. 856,
104 S.Ct. 174, 78 L.Ed.2d 157 (1983); _United States v. Busic,_ 592 F.2d 13, 21 (2d
Cir.1978); _United States v. Bohle,_ 445 F.2d 54, 60 (7th Cir.1971). In light of these
decisions, and absent any encouragement from Congress, we decline Yunis'
invitation to graft a specific intent requirement onto the Antihijacking Act.

Yunis' claim that the Hostage Taking Act requires specific intent also fails. The
statutory language suggests no intent requirement other than that the offender
must act with the purpose of influencing some third person or government
through the hostage taking, a point on which the jury received proper instructions.
See Instructions at 17 (quoting 18 U.S.C. § 1203(a)). Nor are we aware of any
legislative history suggesting that Congress meant to impose a specific intent
requirement. Thus, we conclude that the trial judge's instructions on this count of
the indictment accorded with law.

We find no merit in Yunis' objection (not raised at trial) that the district court
failed to instruct the jury that specific intent is a necessary element of the crime of
conspiracy. True, "the specific intent required for the crime of conspiracy is in fact
the intent to advance or further the unlawful object of the conspiracy." _United
States v. Haldeman,_ 559 F.2d 31, 112 (D.C.Cir.1976) (footnote omitted), _cert. denied,_
431 U.S. 933, 97 S.Ct. 2641, 53 L.Ed.2d 250 (1977). But the jury received instructions that the government "must show beyond a reasonable doubt that the conspiracy was knowingly formed and that the defendant willfully participated in the
unlawful plan with the intent to advance or further some object or purpose of the
conspiracy." Instructions at 10. We discern no defect in this instruction.
*1097 **140 Yunis further contends that, whatever level of criminal intent was
required for these offenses, the district court failed to sufficiently articulate the
government's burden of proving that intent. Because this alternative claim was not
raised at trial, Yunis must show "plain error." Fed.R.Crim.P. 52. The instructions,
however, made it abundantly clear that the government had the burden of proving

the requisite intent beyond a reasonable doubt. *See* Instructions at 10 (conspiracy charge), 17-18 (hostage taking), 27 (general instructions on willfulness and burden of proof). There was no error.

2. Obedience to Military Orders

The final issues before us concern jury instructions relating to Yunis' affirmative defense of obedience to military orders. Yunis and the government agree on the elements of this common law defense, which are established by several civilian court decisions of rather ancient vintage and by military practice. These precedents generally accord with a formulation approved by the Court of Military Appeals in *United States v. Calley,* 22 C.M.A. 534, 48 C.M.R. 19 (1973):

The acts of a subordinate done in compliance with an unlawful order given him by his superior are excused and impose no criminal liability upon him unless the superior's order is one which a man of ordinary sense and understanding would, under the circumstances, know to be unlawful, or if the order in question is actually known to the accused to be unlawful.

Id. at 542, 48 C.M.R. at 27 (opinion of Quinn, J.) (emphasis deleted); *see United States v. Clark,* 31 F. 710, 716-17 (C.C.E.D. Mich.1987); *McCall v. McDowell,* 15 F.Cas. 1235, 1240 (C.C.D. Cal.1867) (No. 8,673); *Neu v. McCarthy,* 309 Mass. 17, 33 N.E.2d 570, 573 (1941); U.S. DEP'T OF DEFENSE, MANUAL FOR COURTS-MARTIAL, UNITED STATES, 1984, R.C.M. 916(d) at II- 128 ("It is a defense to any offense that the accused was acting pursuant to orders unless the accused knew the orders to be unlawful or a person of ordinary sense and understanding would have known the orders to be unlawful.").

Appellant does not disagree with the district court's jury instructions on the general elements of this affirmative defense. Instead, Yunis claims that the district court erred as a matter of law when it instructed the jury that Yunis could prevail on this defense only if the Amal Militia—to which Yunis belonged and which, he claimed, ordered the hijacking—is a "military organization." The court further instructed the jury that it could find that the Amal Militia is a military organization only if the group has a hierarchical command structure and "[c]onducts its operations in accordance with the laws and customs of war," and if its members have a uniform and carry arms openly. Instructions at 34.

 Yunis disputes the district court's position that members of a legitimate military organization must have a uniform. Since the hijackers wore civilian clothes and there was evidence that members of the Amal Militia often dressed this way, appellant concludes that the instruction was prejudicial to his defense. Yunis argues that the relevance of uniforms to the ultimate factual question of whether or not the Amal Militia is a military organization is itself a factual question for the jury, not a question of law. He notes that U.S. courts have not developed any test for determining whether or not defendants who invoke the obedience defense actually belong to bona fide military organizations. But the government responds that courts have not developed such a test simply because the issue has not arisen in U.S. courts; heretofore, the defense has been raised only by members of the United States armed forces. In the government's view, the district court properly adapted its instructions on the obedience defense when faced with novel factual circumstances.

We agree that the district court did not commit legal error when it looked beyond domestic precedents to give jurors guidance in evaluating the Amal Militia's military credentials. Moreover, we find that the test of a bona fide military organization adopted by the district court reflects inter *1098 **141 national practice, providing assurance that Yunis did not suffer from parochial projection of American norms onto the issue of whether he should be treated as a soldier for purposes of the obedience defense.

Specifically, the district court's uniform instruction finds sufficient support in international agreements that bear on the question. *See* Geneva Convention Relative to the Treatment of Prisoners of War, *opened for signature* Aug. 12, 1949, art. 4(A)(2), 6 U.S.T. 3317, 3320, T.I.A.S. No. 3364 [hereinafter Geneva Convention]; Hague Convention No. IV Respecting the Law and Customs of War on Land, Oct. 18, 1907, annex § I, ch. I, art. 1, 36 Stat. 2277, 2295-96, T.S. No. 539 [hereinafter Hague Convention No. IV]. The Geneva Convention, signed by 167 nations including the United States and Lebanon, establishes "having a fixed and distinctive signal recognizable at a distance" as one of four necessary conditions that qualify the members of a militia for treatment as prisoners of war. *See* 6 U.S.T. at 3320. The Hague Convention No. IV, to which the United States and forty-two other nations are parties, uses having "a fixed distinctive emblem recognizable at a distance" as a test for whether militiamen and members of volunteer corps have the rights and responsibilities of national armies. *See* 36 Stat. at 2295-96. At oral argument, counsel for appellant disavowed reliance on the district court's substitution of "uniform" for "signal" or "emblem," and we agree that this free interpretation of the treaty language did not prejudice the defense.

Yunis' second objection to the district court's "military organization" test relates to the instruction, tracking language found in article 4 of the Geneva Convention and chapter I of the annex to the Hague Convention No. IV, that militias must "conduct [their] operations in accordance with the laws and customs of war" to qualify as military organizations. Instructions at 34. Appellant alleges that this instruction must be considered in tandem with the trial judge's statement to the jury that the hijacking of Flight 402 violated international law. Together, he says, these instructions directed the jury to conclude that the defense of obedience to military orders was unavailable to Yunis because no organization could have given the instruction to hijack Flight 402 without violating "the laws and customs of war."

We disagree with appellant's reading of the record, however, and find that when the district court's instructions are considered as a whole, it is highly improbable that a reasonable juror would have understood them to direct a verdict on the affirmative defense. *See United States v. Lemire*, 720 F.2d 1327, 1339 (D.C.Cir.1983), *cert. denied*, 467 U.S. 1226, 104 S.Ct. 2678, 81 L.Ed.2d 874 (1984). In the first place, appellant ignores the trial judge's charge to the jury that it was responsible for determining, based on the evidence, whether or not the Amal Militia is a military organization. Instructions at 34. So too, the court told jurors that if they found that Yunis was a soldier in a military organization under the definition given them, they would then have to address the issue of whether or not Yunis knew that his orders were illegal. *Id.* at 35. Both of these instructions contradict appellant's suggested reading, leading us to conclude that the jury would not have understood the question of whether or not the Amal Militia is a military organization to be foreclosed.

Appellant's interpretation becomes even more attenuated in light of the government's closing argument, during which the prosecution told jurors that they would have to determine whether the Amal Militia is "a military organization that *basically* plays by the rules." Trial Transcript, March 9, 1989, at 106-07 (emphasis added). *See United States v. Park,* 421 U.S. 658, 674-75 & n. 16, 95 S.Ct. 1903, 1912 & n. 16, 44 L.Ed.2d 489 (1975) (jury instructions must be viewed in context of trial as a whole). This statement framed the issue correctly, albeit informally, providing additional assurance that any ambiguity arising from the court's juxtaposition of the illegality instruction and the adherence to international law instruction did not prejudice Yunis' defense. Because the jury instructions, read as a whole and in light of the *1099 **142 evidence and arguments at trial, leave us confident that no prejudicial error occurred, we find that the district court acted within the scope of its discretion.

III. CONCLUSION

For the foregoing reasons, the convictions are
Affirmed.
C.A.D.C.,1991.

DOCUMENT No. 9

UNITED STATES DISTRICT COURT SOUTHERN DISTRICT OF NEW YORK UNITED STATES OF AMERICA

- V-

USAMA BIN LADEN, a/k/a "Usamah Bin-Muhammad Bin-Laden," a/k/a "Shaykh Usamah Bin-Laden," a/k/a "Mujahid Shaykh," a/k/a "Abu Abdallah," a/k/a "Qa Qa,"

Defendant

COUNT ONE

Conspiracy to Attack Defense Utilities of the United States

The Grand Jury charges:

Background: Al Qaeda

1. At all relevant times from in or about 1989 until the date of the filing of this Indictment, an international terrorist group existed which was dedicated to opposing non-Islamic governments with force and violence. This organization grew out of the "mekhtab al Khidemat" (the "Services Office") organization which had maintained (and continues to maintain) offices in various parts of the world, including Afghanistan, Pakistan (particularly in Peshawar) and the United States, particularly at the Alkifah Refugee Center - in Brooklyn. From in or about 1989 until the present, the group called itself "Al Qaeda" ("the Base"). From 1989 until in or about 1991, the group was headquartered in Afghanistan and Peshawar, Pakistan. In or about 1992, the leadership of Al Qaeda, including its "emir" (or prince) USAMA BIN LADEN the defendant, and its military command relocated to the Sudan. From in or about 1991 until the present, the group also called itself the "Islamic Army." The international terrorist group (hereafter referred to as "Al Qaeda") was headquartered in the Sudan from approximately 1992 until approximately 1996 but still maintained offices in various parts of the world. In 1996, USAMA BIN LADEN and Al Qaeda relocated to Afghanistan. At all relevant times, Al Qaeda was led by its "emir," USAMA BIN LADEN. Members of Al Qaeda pledged an oath of allegiance to USAMA BIN LADEN and Al Qaeda.

2. Al Qaeda opposed the United States for several reasons. First, the United States was regarded as "infidel" because it was not governed in a manner consistent with

the group's extremist interpretation of Islam. Second, the United States was viewed as providing essential support for other "infidel" governments and institutions, particularly the governments of Saudi Arabia and Egypt, the nation of Israel and the United Nations, which were regarded as enemies of the group. Third, Al Qaeda opposed the involvement of the United states armed forces in the Gulf War in 1991 and in Operation Restore Hope in Somalia in 1992 and 1993. In particular, Al Qaeda opposed the continued presence of American military forces in Saudi Arabia (and elsewhere on the Saudi Arabian peninsula) following the Gulf war. Fourth, Al Qaeda opposed the United States Government because of the arrest, conviction and imprisonment of persons belonging to Al Qaeda or its affiliated terrorist groups, including Sheik Omar Abdel Rahman.

3. Al Qaeda has functioned both on its own and through some of the terrorist organizations that have operated under its umbrella, including: the Islamic Group (also known as "al Gamaa Islamia" or simply "Gamaa't"), led by co-conspirator Sheik Oxar Abdal Rahman; the al Jihad group based in Egypt; the "Talah e Fatah" ("Vanguards of conquest") faction of al Jibad, which was also based in Egypt, Which faction was led by co-conspirator Ayman al Zawahiri ("al Jibad"); Palestinian Islamic Jihad and a number of Jihad groups in other countries, including Egypt, the Sudan, Saudi Arabia, Yemen, Somalia, Eritrea, Kenya, Pakistan, Bosnia, Croatia, Algeria, Tunisia, Lebanon, the Philippines, Tajikistan, Chechnya, Bangladesh, Kashmir and Azerbaijan. In February 1998, Al Qaeda joined forces with Gamaa't, Al Jihad, the Jihad Movement in Bangladesh and the "Jamaat ul Ulema e Pakistan" to issue a fatwah (an Islamic religious ruling) declaring war against American civilians worldwide under the banner of the "International Islamic Front for Jibad on the Jews and Crusaders."

4. Al Qaeda also forged alliances with the National Islamic Front in the Sudan and with the government of Iran and its associated terrorist group Hezballah for the purpose of working together against their perceived common enemies in the West, particularly the United States. In addition, al Qaeda reached an understanding with the government of Iraq that al Qaeda would not work against that government and that on particular projects, specifically including weapons development, al Qaeda would work cooperatively with the Government of Iraq.

5. Al Qaeda had a command and control structure which included a majlis al shura (or consultation council) which discussed and approved major undertakings, including terrorist operations.

6. Al Qaeda also conducted internal investigations of its members and their associates in an effort to detect informants and killed those suspected of collaborating with enemies of Al Qaeda.

7. From at least 1991 until the date of the filing of this Indictment, in the Sudan, Afghanistan and elsewhere out of the jurisdiction of any particular state or district, USAMA BIN LADEN, a/k/a "Usamah Bin-Muhammad Bin-Laden," a/k/a

"Shaykh Usamah Bin-Laden," a/k/a "Mujahid Shaykh," a/k/a "Abu Abdallah," a/k/a "Qa Qa," the defendant, and a co-conspirator not named as a defendant herein (hereafter "Co-conspirator") who was first brought to and arrested in the Southern District of New York, and others known and unknown to the grand jury, unlawfully, willfully and knowingly combined conspired, confederated and agreed together and with each other to injure and destroy, and attempt to injure and destroy, national-defense material, national-defense premises and national-defense utilities of the United States with the intent to injure, interfere with and obstruct the national defense of the United states.

Overt Acts

8. In furtherance of the said conspiracy, and to effect the illegal object thereof, the following overt acts, among others, were committed:

a. At various times from at least as early as 1991 until at least in or about February 1998, USAMA BIN LADEN, the defendant, met with Co-conspirator and other members of Al Qaeda in the Sudan, Afghanistan and elsewhere;

b. At various times from at least as early as 1991, USAMA BIN LADEN, and others known and unknown, made efforts to obtain weapons, including firearms and explosives, for Al Qaeda and its affiliated terrorist groups;

c. At various times from at least as early as 1991 USAMA BIN LADEN, and others known and unknown, provided training camps and guest houses in various areas, including Afghanistan and the Sudan, for the use of Al Qaeda and its affiliated terrorist groups;

d. At various times from at least as early as 1991, USAMA BIN LADEN, and others known and unknown, made efforts to produce counterfeit passports purporting to be issued by various countries and also obtained official passports from the Government of the Sudan for use by Al Qaeda and its affiliated groups;

e. At various times from at least as early as 1991, USAMA BIN LADEN, and others known and unknown, made efforts to recruit United States citizens to Al Qaeda in order to utilize the American citizens for travel throughout the Western world to deliver messages and engage in financial transactions for the benefit of Al Qaeda and its affiliated groups;

f. At various times from at least as early as 1991, USAMA BIN LADEN, and others known and unknown, made efforts to utilize non-Government organizations which purported to be engaged in humanitarian work as conduits for transmitting funds for the benefit of Al Qaeda and its affiliated groups;

g. At various times from at least as early as 1991, Co-conspirator and others known and unknown to the grand jury engaged in financial and business transactions on behalf of defendant USAMA BIN LADEN and Al Qaeda, including, but not limited to: purchasing land for training camps; purchasing warehouses for storage of items, including explosives; transferring funds between bank accounts opened in various names, obtaining various communications equipment, including satellite telephones and transporting currency and weapons to members of Al Qaeda and its associated terrorist organizations in various countries throughout the world;

h. At various times from in or about 1992 until the date of the filing of this Indictment, USAMA BIN LADEN and other ranking members of Al Qaeda stated privately to other members of Al Qaeda that Al Qaeda should put aside its differences with Shiite Muslim terrorist organizations, including the Government of Iran and its affiliated terrorist group Hezballah, to cooperate against the perceived common enemy, the United States and its allies;

i. At various times from in or about 1992 until the date of the filing of this Indictment, USAMA BIN LADEN and other ranking members of Al Qaeda stated privately to other members of Al Qaeda that the United States forces stationed on the Saudi Arabian peninsula, including both Saudi Arabia and Yemen, should be Attacked;

j. At various times from in or about 1992 until the date of the filing of this Indictment, USAMA BIN LADEN and other ranking members of Al Qaeda stated privately to other members of Al Qaeda that the United States forces stationed in the Horn of Africa, including Somalia, should be attacked;

k. Beginning in or about early spring 1993, Al Qaeda members began to provide training and assistance to Somali tribes opposed to the United Nations intervention in Somalia;

l. On October 3 and 4, 1993, members of Al Qaeda participated with Somali tribesmen in an attack on United States military personnel serving in Somalia as part of Operation Restore Hope, which attack killed a total of 18 United States soldiers and wounded 73 others in Mogadishu;

m. On two occasions in the period from in or about 1992 until in or about 1995, Co-conspirator helped transport weapons and explosives from Khartoum to Port Sudan for transshipment to the Saudi Arabian peninsula;

n. At various times from at least as early as 1993, USAMA BIN LADEN and others known and unknown, made efforts to obtain the components of nuclear weapons;

o. At various times from at least as early as 1993 USAMA BIN LADEN and others known and unknown, made efforts to produce chemical weapons;

p. On or about August 23, 1996, USAMA BIN LADEN signed and issued a declaration of Jihad entitled "Message from Usamah Bin-Muhammad Bin-Laden to His Muslim Brothers in the Whole World and Especially in the Arabian Peninsula:

Declaration of Jihad Against the Americans Occupying the Land of the Two Holy Mosques; Expel the Heretics from the Arabian Peninsula" (hereafter the "Declaration of Jihad) from the Hindu Kush mountains in Afghanistan. The Declaration of Jihad included statements that efforts should be pooled to kill Americans and encouraged other persons to join the jihad against the American enemy";

q. In or about late August 1996, USAMA BIN LADEN read aloud the Declaration of Jihad and made an audiotape recording of such reading for worldwide distribution; and

r. In February 1998, USAMA BIN LADEN issued a joint declaration in the name of Gamaa't, Al Jihad, the Jihad movement in Bangladesh and the "Jamaat ul Ulema e Pakistan" under the banner of the "International Islamic Front for Jihad on the Jews and Crusaders," which stated that Muslims should kill Americans — including civilians — anywhere in the world where they can be found.

DOCUMENT No. 10

Lockerbie Verdict

Edited text of the verdict against Abdel Basset Ali al-Megrahi of Libya in the bombing of Pan Am Flight 103 over Lockerbie, Scotland on December 21, 1988.

January 31, 2001

IN THE HIGH COURT OF JUSTICIARY AT CAMP ZEIST

Lord Sutherland
Lord Coulsfield

Lord MacLean   Case No: 1475/99

OPINION OF THE COURT
delivered by LORD SUTHERLAND
in causa
HER MAJESTY'S ADVOCATE

v

ABDELBASET ALI MOHMED AL MEGRAHI and AL AMIN KHALIFA
FHIMAH, Prisoners in the Prison of Zeist, Camp Zeist (Kamp van Zeist), The
Netherlands

Accused

[1] At 1903 hours on 22 December 1988 PanAm flight 103 fell out of the sky. The 259 passengers and crew members who were on board and 11 residents of Lockerbie where the debris fell were killed. The Crown case is that the cause of the disaster was that an explosive device had been introduced into the hold of the aircraft by the two accused whether acting alone or in concert with each other and others. This device exploded when the aircraft was in Scottish air space thus causing the aircraft to disintegrate. In these circumstances it was originally contended that the accused were guilty of conspiracy to murder, alternatively murder, alternatively a contravention of section 2(1) and (5) of the Aviation Security Act 1982. At the conclusion of the Crown's submissions, however, the libel was restricted to the charge of murder.

[2] It is not disputed, and was amply proved, that the cause of the disaster was indeed the explosion of a device within the aircraft. Nor is it disputed that the person or persons who were responsible for the deliberate introduction of the explosive device would be guilty of the crime of murder. The matter at issue in this trial therefore is whether or not the Crown have proved beyond reasonable doubt that one or other or both of the accused was responsible, actor or art and part, for the deliberate introduction of the device.

[3] After the disaster a massive police operation was mounted to recover as much as possible of the debris in order to ascertain the cause of the crash. Tens of thousands of items were recovered, sifted and recorded, and any that appeared to be of particular interest as indicating a possible cause of the explosion were examined by the relevant specialists.

[4] All the parts of the aircraft that were recovered were taken initially to a hangar in Longtown where they were examined by inspectors of the Air Accidents Investigation Board ("AAIB"). Subsequently the relevant part of the aircraft was reconstructed as far as possible at Farnborough. It was found that the majority of the fractures in the skin of the fuselage were overload fractures consistent with the type of damage to be expected from the airborne break-up of an aircraft structure. There was however an area where the fracture failure characteristics were not typical. This area was on the port side of the lower fuselage in the forward cargo bay area. The basic structure of the aircraft consisted of substantial vertical frames set 20" apart and horizontal stringers about 10" apart, with the fuselage skin being attached to the outside. A small region of the structure bounded approximately by frames 700 and 720 and stringers 38 left and 40 left, thus approximately 20" square, had been completely shattered. The fractures around the shattered area were granular in character, whereas further away the fractures were typical tearing fractures. Around the shattered area there were signs of pitting and sooting. The skin panels in the area immediately surrounding the shattered area had been bent and torn in a starburst pattern and were petalled outwards. From the nature of this damage the conclusion was reached, and it is one which we accept, that the cause of the damage was the detonation of an explosive device within the fuselage, with the initial shattered area forming the focus for the subsequent petalling mode of failure. Further processes led on from that which caused the total disruption and disintegration of the aircraft.

[5] The port side forward cargo bay was loaded with luggage in containers. These containers were approximately 5' by 5' by 5', with an overhang of approximately 18" angled up from the base on the outboard side designed to make maximum use of the curved space in the cargo hold. Most of the containers were made of aluminium apart from the after side which was open for loading and then covered by a plastic curtain. A few of the containers were made of glass-reinforced fibre. The containers were loaded on to the aircraft through a door in the hold, and then slid on rollers into a prearranged position where they were clamped. As part of the reconstruction process, the recovered pieces of containers were reassembled, principally by Mr Claiden, an engineering inspector with the AAIB. When this was done, it was ascertained that with two exceptions there was no damage to containers other than was to be expected from the disintegration of the aircraft and the containers' fall to the ground. It was however found that there was unusual damage to an aluminium container AVE 4041 and a fibre container AVN 7511. From the loading plan of the containers it was ascertained that AVE 4041 was situated immediately inboard of and slightly above the shattered area of the fuselage, and AVN 7511 was situated immediately aft of AVE 4041. The reconstruction of AVE 4041 demonstrated severe damage to the floor panel and outboard base frame member in the outboard aft quadrant, and also on the

internal aspect of that part of the container there were some areas of blackening and pitting. There was also damage to the panels and frame members at the lower aft side of the overhang, and again areas of blackening and pitting. The full details of the nature and extent of the damage are to be found in the evidence of Mr Claiden, and are confirmed in the evidence of Dr Hayes and Mr Feraday, forensic scientists with the Royal Armaments Research and Development Establishment ("RARDE"). The nature of the damage indicated a high-energy event, and the sooting and pitting indicated an explosion. Mr Claiden, whose evidence was given in an impressively careful and restrained manner, stated "I have no doubts in my mind that such an event occurred from within the container", the only occasion on which he stated an absolutely unqualified opinion. Because of the distribution of the areas of sooting and pitting, and in particular the absence of any such signs on the base of the container, it appeared to Mr Claiden that, assuming that an explosive device was contained in a piece of luggage in the container, the likelihood was that that piece of luggage was not lying on the floor of the container but was lying probably on top of a case on the floor and projecting into the overhang of the container. Ascertainment of the precise location of the explosive device was assisted by consideration of the damage to the adjacent container AVN 7511. The forward face of that container had a hole approximately 8" square about 10" up from the top of the base radiating out from which were areas of sooting extending up to the top of the container. This indicated that a relatively mild blast had exited AVE 4041 and impinged at an angle on the forward face of AVN 7511. Combining that information with the damage to AVE 4041, the likely position of an explosive device was about 13" above the floor of AVE 4041. On that assumption allied to the previous assumption that the piece of luggage containing the device was projecting into the overhang, the position of the device would be approximately 25" from the skin of the fuselage. We found the evidence of Mr Claiden wholly credible, reliable and compelling so far as it went. He was not however an expert on explosives or the effects of explosives. The conclusion reached by Dr Hayes and Mr Feraday as to the position of the explosive device coincided with that of Mr Claiden, and in addition Mr Feraday was present at tests in the USA. Thtests involved the use of luggage filled metal containers and the placing of plastic explosives within Toshiba radio cassette players in a garment filled suitcase. The tests confirmed the opinion he expressed as to the position of the explosive device and the quantity of explosive involved.

[6] Technical evidence relating to the effects of explosives was given by Dr Cullis and Professor Peel. Dr Cullis is an expert on the effects of blast and the development of computer codes to simulate the effects of blast in particular different situations, and has been employed at the Defence Evaluation and Research Agency ("DERA") since 1978. Professor Peel is the chief scientist for DERA, specialising in materials and structures used in aircraft, and leader of a team conducting research into *interalia* the assessment of the effect of detonation of explosives in aircraft. They confirmed that the presence of pitting and carbon deposits which would look like a very fine soot indicated a chemical explosion. The areas in which this would occur would have to be in line of sight with the explosive, and in particular, as far as pitting was con-

cerned, there would have to be no intervening structure of sufficient mass to prevent explosive fragments impacting on the pitted area. The nature of the cracking in the floor panel of the container is typical of the sort of deformation which would be seen from blast loading, but the absence of pitting or sooting in that area would indicate that there must have been something such as another suitcase situated between the explosive device and the floor panel. On the other hand the pitting and sooting seen on the inner aspect of the horizontal base frame member of the container combined with downward deformation of that member confirms the view that the explosive device was situated above and in direct line of sight of that member and thus was likely to be situated partly at least in the overhang where the presence of a suitcase on the floor of the container would not inhibit the explosive products from striking that member. Further confirmation of the position of the explosive device came from the observation of crushing to the upper surface of the aircraft fuselage frame 700 and pitting and sooting of the two neighbouring frames, this being the area adjacent to the lower after end of the container. Professor Peel's evidence also included a substantial complex section on the nature of impulse loading, the critical level of impulse for failure of aluminium alloy sheet of the type used for the fuselage skin, and the calculation of both the stand-off distance and the size of the explosive charge from the size of the shattered zone and the petalled zone. These calculations indicated a charge of about 450 grammes and a stand-off distance of 610 millimetres, which would take the explosion 200 millimetres inside the container. We do not consider it necessary to go into detail about these complex calculations, as the physical evidence of damage to the hull, the container, and, as we shall see later, the contents of the container satisfies us beyond any doubt that the explosion occurred within the container, and the calculations serve merely to confirm that view. We should add that this section of his evidence also dealt with the effect, if any, of the concept of Mach stem formation, but we do not consider it necessary to go into any detail about that, as we accept his evidence that although that concept was considered as a means of assessing stand-off distance, it was not actually used.

****

[8] From this evidence we are entirely satisfied that the cause of the disaster was the explosion of a device which was contained within the aircraft. We would also be satisfied that the device was within container AVE 4041, but any possible doubts about that would be dispelled by the evidence relating to the examination of the apparent contents of that container, to which we now turn.

[9] During the course of the massive ground search, a large quantity of luggage and clothing was collected and labelled. Within a few days of the disaster it was established that an explosion had occurred, and accordingly the searchers were asked in particular to recover any items which appeared to be scorched or blackened or otherwise had the appearance of having been involved in an explosion. Any such items were then submitted to the Forensic Explosives Laboratory at RARDE for detailed examination, the principal forensic scientists involved being Dr Hayes and Mr Feraday. Fifty-six fragments which showed various signs of explosives damage were identified

as forming part of what had been a brown hardshell Samsonite suitcase of the 26" Silhouette 4000 range ("the primary suitcase"). The nature of the damage indicated that it had been inflicted from within the suitcase. A further twenty-four items of luggage were identified by their characteristic explosives damage as having been in relatively close proximity to the explosive device. Within many of these items there were found fragments of what appeared to be parts of the primary suitcase, and also fragments of what appeared to have been a radio cassette player. Other similar fragments were found in clothing which from their charred appearance were considered to have been contained in the primary suitcase. In addition, when examining a data plate which had been attached to AVE 4041, Mr Claiden recovered a piece of debris which appeared to be a small piece of circuit board. The number of fragments associated with the clothing in close contact with the explosion and the extent of the shattering of these fragments indicated that the charge had in all probability been located within the radio. It was known at that time that in October 1988 the West German police had recovered a Toshiba radio cassette player which had been modified to form an improvised explosive device. Mr Feraday visited West Germany to examine this device, and ascertained that the fragments in his possession and in particular the piece of circuit board recovered by Mr Claiden did not originate from the same model. However, he considered that there was a sufficient similarity to make it worth investigating other models of Toshiba players. It was found that there were seven models in which the printed circuit board bore precisely the same characteristics as the fragments. Subsequently, when the blast damaged clothing was examined in detail there were found embedded in two different Slalom brand shirts, a Babygro, and a pair of tartan checked trousers, fragments of paper which on examination proved to be from an owner's manual for a Toshiba RT-SF 16 BomBeat radio cassette player. All the other fragments thought to have originated from the radio containing the explosive were consistent with having come from an RT-SF 16. Other fragments of plastic associated with the radio were found in other items of clothing considered to have been in the primary suitcase, namely a white T-shirt, cream pyjamas, a herringbone jacket, and brown herringbone trousers, as well as in the four items in which the fragments of paper were found. The conclusion reached by the forensic scientists was that the nature of the fragments and their distribution left no doubt that the explosive charge was contained within the Toshiba radio, and we agree with that conclusion. Having regard to the presence of fragments of an RT-SF 16 owner's manual, we also accept that it was that model of Toshiba radio that was involved.

[10] As we have noted, a substantial quantity of clothing was examined at RARDE. The primary concern was to ascertain what clothing showed signs of explosion damage, and then, if possible, to differentiate between clothing likely to have been contained within the suitcase that contained the explosive device and clothing in adjacent suitcases. The method adopted by the forensic scientists was to treat as a high probability that any explosion damaged clothing which contained fragments of the radio cassette player, the instruction manual, and the brown fabric-lined cardboard partition from within the suitcase to the exclusion of fragments of the outer shell, was within the primary suitcase. Where clothing carried neither fragments of the explosive device nor of one or more of the suitcase shells that would have surrounded

it, or where it variously carried fragments of the suitcase shells with or without fragments of the explosive device, its specific location was problematic, although the possibility that it was contained in the primary suitcase could not be discounted. There were twelve items of clothing and an umbrella of which fragments were recovered and examined which fell within the first category and accordingly in their opinion had been contained within the primary suitcase. These items were:-

1. A charred fragment of white cotton material which from the details of the stitching and method of assembly appeared most likely to have originated from a white T-shirt of Abanderado brand. Contained within this fragment there were found a piece of loudspeaker mesh and eleven plastic fragments which could have come from a Toshiba radio, and some blue/white fragments consistent with having come from a Babygro (see item 5).

2. Explosion damaged fragments of brown tartan patterned material two of which still retained parts of labels which identified them as having formed part of a pair of Yorkie brand trousers size 34. Contained within one of these fragments there were found fragments of the lining and internal divider of the primary suitcase, five black plastic fragments which could have come from a Toshiba radio, four fragments of an RT-SF 16 owner's manual, and five clumps of blue/white fibres consistent with having come from a Babygro.

3. Four charred and disrupted fragments of grey cloth which in terms of colour, weave and texture appeared to have a common origin. One of these fragments had sewn on to it a "Slalom" label, and all the fragments were consistent with having come from a grey Slalom brand shirt. Contained within one of these fragments (bearing the police label PI/995) there were found a number of items. We shall return to this fragment later, as the defence contended that there were a number of factors surrounding its finding and examination which affected the reliability of the evidence relating to it.

4. Six charred fragments of white material with a fine blue pin-stripe. Although there were no identifying marks on any of these fragments, their colour, weave, texture and construction indicated that their origin was from a shirt closely similar to a Slalom brand shirt. Contained within these fragments there were found sixteen fragments of black plastic and four fragments of loudspeaker mesh which could have come from a Toshiba radio and fragments of an RT-SF 16 owner's manual.

5. Four explosion-damaged fragments of light brown herringbone woven cloth. Although there were no identifying marks on any of these fragments, their colour, weave, texture and construction indicated that their origin was from a pair of Yorkie brand trousers. Six pieces of black plastic and a fragment of the divider of the primary suitcase were found contained therein.

6. Three explosion-damaged fragments of herringbone patterned brown tweed cloth. Although there were no identifying marks on any of these

fragments, their colour, weave, texture and construction indicated that their origin was from a tweed jacket similar in all respects to a control sample obtained by police officers. These fragments contained fragments of black plastic and suitcase divider.

7. Four fragments of cream coloured material with a pattern of brown stripes. One of these was a substantial item clearly identifiable as the remains of a pair of pyjama trousers. Although there were no identifying marks on any of these fragments, their colour, pattern and construction indicated that their origin was from a pair of Panwear brand pyjamas. They contained fragments of black plastic and fragments of lining from the primary suitcase.

8. Thirteen very severely damaged fragments, many extremely small, of blue fibrous material. One fragment consisted of two overlaid pieces of material, one being a blue fibrous material and the other being knitted white ribbed material. Between these two pieces there was trapped the remains of a label printed in different colours containing information about age, height, composition and "made in Malta". This composite fragment matched closely in all significant respects the labelled neck section of a Babygro Primark brand. The material of the other fragments also matched the material of the same brand. Adhering to these various fragments were fragments of black plastic, wire, paper fragments from the Toshiba owner's manual, and fragments of the divider of the primary suitcase.

9. Three fragments of a black nylon umbrella. The major fragments comprised part of the canopy, ribbing and handle stem, shredded and partly collapsed indicating close involvement with an explosion. Strongly adherent to the canopy material were blue and white fibres, similar in appearance to the Babygro fibres. A second fragment was a piece of silver coated black plastic with fluted surface corrugations similar to part of the locking collar of the umbrella, and this was found in a fragment of the tartan checked trousers (item 2 above).

10. A fragment of an explosion damaged knitted brown woollen cardigan. This item had sewn on to it a label inscribed "Puccini design".
    The remaining three items had clearly been very closely involved with the explosion, but there was insufficient material to enable identification to be made of their origin.

[11] The nature and extent of the damage to this clothing together with the items embedded confirmed, if confirmation were necessary, that the explosion had occurred within container AVE 4041, and also established beyond doubt that the explosive device was contained within a Toshiba RT-SF 16 radio cassette player which had been within a brown Samsonite suitcase which also contained the items of clothing enumerated above.

[12] It will be recalled that four of the items identified as having been in the primary suitcase were identifiable by labels as having been of Yorkie, Slalom, Primark and

Puccini brands. In August 1989 police officers visited Malta in an attempt to trace the source of these items. After a visit to Yorkie Clothing, on 1 September they went to Mary's House, Tower Road, Sliema. This was a shop run by the Gauci family, Tony Gauci being one of the partners. Mr Gauci's evidence was that he was visited by police officers in September 1989. He was able to tell them that he recalled a particular sale about a fortnight before Christmas 1988, although he could not remember the exact date. His recollection was that the Christmas lights were just being put up. It was midweek, possibly Wednesday. The time was about 6.30pm. The purchaser was a man, and the witness recognised him as being a Libyan. The conversation with the purchaser was probably in a mixture of Arabic, English and Maltese. Many Libyans visit his shop, and when he hears them speaking he can tell the difference between a Libyan and, say, a Tunisian or an Egyptian. He bought an assortment of clothing, but it did not appear to the witness that the nature of what he was buying was of importance. Amongst the items which the witness remembered selling were two pairs of Yorkie trousers, two pairs of striped pyjamas of the same brand as the Panwear fragment, a tweed jacket, a blue Babygro, two Slalom shirts collar size 16½ , two cardigans, one brown and one blue, and an umbrella. The order number seen on the fragment of one of the pairs of Yorkie trousers was 1705, and the delivery note for this order showed that it was delivered on 18 November 1988. The police obtained either from Mr Gauci or from the manufacturers samples of all of these items, and these were the samples which were used by the forensic scientists when comparing them with the fragments. It may seem surprising that he was able to remember this particular sale in such detail some nine months afterwards, but he explained that the purchaser appeared to be taking little interest in the items he was buying. We are satisfied, however, that his recollection of these items is accurate. While it was never suggested to him that his recollection might have been assisted by the police officers, it is perhaps a measure of his accuracy that he was clear that the purchases did not include an Abanderado T-shirt, even though he did stock such items and it would be one in which the police were interested. While no doubt individual items could have been purchased in many other shops in Malta, or indeed in other parts of the world as many of them were exported, the exact match between so many of the items and the fragments found at Lockerbie is in our view far more than just a coincidence. We are therefore entirely satisfied that the items of clothing in the primary suitcase were those described by Mr Gauci as having been purchased in Mary's House. We shall return to Mr Gauci's evidence in more detail in connection with the date of the sale and the identification of the purchaser.

****

[14] Over the ensuing months extensive investigations were carried out by CI Williamson and other police officers within the printed circuit board industry in an attempt to trace the origin of the fragment, but these were fruitless. In about June 1990 CI Williamson received information from an FBI officer named Thurman as a result of which he and Mr Feraday visited FBI headquarters in Washington. They were there shown a timing device known as an MST-13 (label 420). On examination it was found that there was an area on a printed circuit board within that timer which

was identical to the recovered fragment except that the Washington device had double-sided solder masking whereas the fragment PT/35(b) was solder masked on one side only. Subsequent enquiries led to a commission rogatoire being obtained, which enabled judicial and police authorities in Switzerland to carry out enquiries on behalf of the Scottish police. In November 1990 and January 1991 there were judicial interviews of two persons, Edwin Bollier and Erwin Meister, the partners in the firm of MEBO, a firm which was engaged in the design and manufacture of various electronic items. There was a further interview with Scottish police officers in May 1991. During the course of these interviews, a number of items were handed over including a quantity of documentation, three timers (two MST-13s and an Olympus), and various components of timers including circuit boards. The detailed examination of these items by Dr Hayes and Mr Feraday and comparison with the fragment of green circuit board left them in no doubt that the fragment originated from an area of the connection pad for an output relay of a circuit board of single solder-mask type of an MST-13 timer. We accept the conclusion to which the forensic scientists came.

[15] The evidence which we have considered up to this stage satisfies us beyond reasonable doubt that the cause of the disaster was the explosion of an improvised explosive device, that that device was contained within a Toshiba radio cassette player in a brown Samsonite suitcase along with various items of clothing, that that clothing had been purchased in Mary's House, Sliema, Malta, and that the initiation of the explosion was triggered by the use of an MST-13 timer.

[16] We now turn to consider the evidence relating to the provenance of the primary suitcase and the possible ways in which it could have found its way into AVE 4041. This involves consideration of the procedures at various airports through which it may have passed.

[17] The Crown case is that the primary suitcase was carried on an Air Malta flight KM180 from Luqa Airport in Malta to Frankfurt, that at Frankfurt it was transferred to PanAm flight PA103A, a feeder flight for PA103, which carried it to London Heathrow Airport, and that there, in turn, it was transferred to PA103. This case is largely dependent on oral and documentary evidence relating to the three airports. From this evidence, it is alleged, an inference can be drawn that an unidentified and unaccompanied item of baggage was carried on KM180 and transferred to PA103A at Frankfurt and PA103 at Heathrow.

[18] When an intending passenger checks in baggage for carriage in an aircraft hold, a numbered tag is attached to each item. Part of the tag is removed and given to the passenger to act as a receipt. The portion attached to the item of baggage bears, ordinarily, the name of the airline, or the first airline, on which the passenger is to travel and the destination. Where the journey is to be completed in more than one leg or stage, the tag also carries the name of any intermediate airport. The purpose of the tag is to enable the baggage handlers at the airport of departure, at any intermediate airport and at the destination to deliver or transfer the item to the correct flight and return it to the passenger at the final destination. In 1988, tags preprinted with the name of the destination airport were sometimes used when the journey was to be

completed in one stage. Where there was more than one stage, the names of the destination and of any intermediate airport were normally written on the tag by hand at the time of check-in. Baggage checked in at the airport of departure is referred to as local origin baggage. Baggage which has to be handled at an intermediate airport is generally referred to as transit baggage. A distinction is normally made between two groups of transit baggage. Online baggage is baggage which arrives at and departs from an intermediate airport on aircraft of the same carrier: interline baggage arrives on an aircraft of one carrier and departs with a different carrier. The terminology is, however, not always used consistently. Baggage is intended to be carried on the same aircraft as the passenger to whom it belongs, but from time to time baggage is misdirected or delayed and has to be carried on a different flight. Such items are identified by an additional special tag, known as a rush tag, and are normally only sent in response to a request from the destination airport, following a claim made by a passenger for baggage which has not been delivered at the destination. The evidence led on this point related only to practice at Luqa airport, but seemed to reflect international practice. A passenger aircraft may also carry items of mail and other freight.

[19] In 1988, and for some time before, airline operators and airport authorities generally were well aware of the risk that attempts might be made to place explosive devices on passenger aircraft and had in place systems intended to minimise that risk. In particular, it was normal to take steps to prevent items of baggage travelling on an aircraft unaccompanied by the passenger who had checked them in, unless there was sufficient reason to regard the items as safe. It was normal to put certain questions to passengers who checked in baggage for a flight and to ensure that every passenger who had checked in baggage at the departure airport had boarded the aircraft, or that safety was otherwise assured, before it was allowed to depart. Similarly, steps were taken to check that transit baggage did not travel without the accompanying passenger. These steps varied between different airports and different carriers. By 1988, PanAm had brought into operation a system of x-raying interline baggage at Frankfurt and Heathrow. The availability of that facility led to changes in the way in which interline passengers and baggage were handled.

[20] PA103 took off from Heathrow shortly before 1830 on 21 December 1988. It was the last transatlantic PanAm flight to depart on that day. Heathrow was therefore the last place at which an explosive device could have been introduced into the hold of the aircraft. Before its departure, the aircraft was parked at stand K14. It had previously been checked and an airworthiness sheet had been completed for it. PA103A arrived at stand K16 and passengers proceeding to New York were instructed to go direct to gate 14. The boarding of passengers, both those originating at Heathrow and those transferring from PA103A, proceeded normally except that one passenger who had checked in two items of baggage at Heathrow failed to appear at the gate. The passenger was an American citizen and a decision was taken that the aircraft could depart despite his non-appearance. It was later found that he had been drinking in a bar at the airport and missed the boarding call. There is no reason to connect that passenger or the items checked in by him with the explosive device.

[21] At Heathrow, as at Frankfurt, PanAm baggage was handled by employees of PanAm. Security duties for PanAm were carried out by employees of Alert Security, an affiliate company of PanAm. Baggage checked in at Heathrow was sent to an area known as the baggage build-up area before taken to the aircraft when it was ready for loading. The build-up area was adjacent to a roadway extensively used by persons within the airport. In December 1988 it was busier than usual because construction work was in progress at the airport. If, as was the case with a Boeing 747 aircraft, the baggage, or any of it, was to be loaded into containers to be placed in the aircraft, that was done in the build-up area. Interline baggage arriving at Heathrow was unloaded by airport employees and was sent to an area called the interline shed. This shed was a separate building within the airport terminal area. Baggage removed from incoming flights was brought to the outside of the shed by employees of a company called Whyte's, employed by the airport authority, and placed on a conveyor belt, which carried it into the shed. There was no security guard outside the shed, so that the placing of items on the conveyor belt was unsupervised. The interline shed dealt with baggage for other airlines, as well as baggage for PanAm. Within the shed, interline baggage for a PanAm flight was identified and separated from other airline baggage. It was taken to the PanAm x-ray machine, where it was examined by x-ray by an employee of Alert. After x-ray, it was placed in a container or set aside to await the outgoing flight.

[22] On 21 December 1988 the x-ray operator was Sulkash Kamboj. John Bedford, a loader-driver employed by PanAm, and Mr Parmar, another PanAm employee were working in the interline shed. Mr Bedford set aside container AVE 4041 to receive interline baggage for PA103. The container was identified as the container for PA103 by Mr Bedford who wrote the information on a sheet which was placed in a holder fixed to the container. A number of items were placed in that container. Later Mr Bedford drove the container to a position near the baggage build-up area and left it there. From there, the container was taken out to stand K16, and baggage for New York unloaded from PA103A was loaded into it. The incoming plane carried baggage loose in its hold, not in containers. The evidence of Mr Bedford together with that of Peter Walker, a supervisor in the baggage build-up area, and Darshan Sandhu, a chief loader, and with the container build-up sheet (production 1217), shows that container AVE 4041 contained both interline baggage which had been placed in it in the interline shed, and baggage unloaded from PA103A. When it was full, container AVE 4041 was driven directly to stand 14 and loaded into the hold. The evidence of Terence Crabtree, another driver-loader employed by PanAm, who was the crew chief for the loading of PA103, together with the load plan (production 1183), shows that the container was loaded in position 14 left, which corresponds to the position established by the forensic evidence. The plan also shows that container AVN 7511 was loaded in the adjacent position 21 left, again corresponding to the forensic evidence. There was also some baggage from PA103A which was loaded loose into the hold of PA103.

[23] Mr Bedford said that he recalled that on 21 December 1988 he had set aside container AVE 4041 for baggage for PA103. He recalled also that he had placed a

number of suitcases in the container. These cases were placed on their spines in a row along the back of the container. He said that he had left the interline shed to have a cup of tea with Mr Walker in the build-up area. On his return, he saw that two cases had been added to the container. These cases were laid on their sides, with the handles towards the interior of the container, in the way that he would normally have loaded them. The arrangement of these cases was shown in a set of photographs (production 1114) taken in early January 1989 in Mr Bedford's presence. Mr Bedford said that he had been told by Mr Kamboj that he had placed the additional two suitcases in the container during his absence. Mr Kamboj denied that he had placed any suitcases in the container and denied also that he had told Mr Bedford that he had done so. Both witnesses were referred to a number of police statements which they gave at various times and to their evidence at the Fatal Accident Inquiry into the disaster, and it appears that each of the witnesses has consistently given the same account throughout. Mr Kamboj eventually conceded in evidence, in a half-hearted way, that what Mr Bedford said might be correct, but the contradiction is not resolved. Mr Bedford was a clear and impressive witness and he had no reason to invent what he said. Mr Kamboj was a less impressive witness, and he might have been anxious to avoid any possible responsibility. In our view, the evidence of Mr Bedford should be preferred on this point. The difference between the witnesses is not, however, material since for the purposes of this case what is important is that there is evidence that when the container left the interline area it had in it the two suitcases positioned as described above. Mr Bedford agreed that in statements to police officers and in evidence at the Fatal Accident Inquiry he had described one of the two cases lying on their sides as a brown or maroony-brown hardshell Samsonite-type case. He could not recollect that when he gave evidence in this case, but said that he had told the truth in his statements and earlier evidence. Mr Bedford also said that he had arranged with Mr Walker that because the incoming flight PA103A was a little delayed, and to wait for it would take him beyond his normal finishing time, he should take the container to the baggage build-up area and leave it there, and that he did so before leaving work soon after 5.00pm. Mr Walker could not recall what had happened, but accepted that he had told investigating police officers soon after the event that he recalled seeing Mr Bedford at about 5.00pm and that Mr Bedford had said that he was going home, but that there was no conversation about leaving a container at the build-up area. Mr Walker's evidence at the FAI in regard to whether or not he was aware of a container being brought to the build-up area differed from his original police statement and he was unable to explain the difference. There is, however, no reason to doubt Mr Bedford's evidence that he did take AVE 4041 to the build-up area and leave it there.

[24] It emerges from the evidence therefore that a suitcase which could fit the forensic description of the primary suitcase was in the container when it left the interline shed. There is also a possibility that an extraneous suitcase could have been introduced by being put onto the conveyor belt outside the interline shed, or introduced into the shed itself or into the container when it was at the build-up area. To achieve that, the person placing the suitcase would have had to avoid being detected, but the evidence indicates that a person in possession of a pass for the airside area would not be likely to be challenged, and there were a very large number of passes issued for

Heathrow, a substantial number of which were not accounted for. The person placing the suitcase would also have required to know where to put it to achieve the objective.

[25] It was argued on behalf of the accused that the suitcase described by Mr Bedford could well have been the primary suitcase, particularly as the evidence did not disclose that any fragments of a hard-shell Samsonite-type suitcase had been recovered, apart from those of the primary suitcase itself. It was accepted, for the purposes of this argument, that the effect of forensic evidence was that the suitcase could not have been directly in contact with the floor of the container. It was submitted that there was evidence that an American Tourister suitcase, which had travelled from Frankfurt, fragments of which had been recovered, had been very intimately involved in the explosion and could have been placed under the suitcase spoken to by Mr Bedford. That would have required rearrangement of the items in the container, but such rearrangement could easily have occurred when the baggage from Frankfurt was being put into the conton the tarmac at Heathrow. It is true that such a rearrangement could have occurred, but if there was such a rearrangement, the suitcase described by Mr Bedford might have been placed at some more remote corner of the container, and while the forensic evidence dealt with all the items recovered which showed direct explosive damage, twenty-five in total, there were many other items of baggage found which were not dealt with in detail in the evidence in the case.

[26] At Frankfurt Airport, baggage for most airlines was handled by the airport authority, but PanAm had their own security and baggage handling staff. Frankfurt had a computer controlled automated baggage handling system, through which baggage was passed. Each item of baggage was placed in an individually numbered tray as it was taken into the system. The trays were placed on conveyor belts and instructions were fed into the computer to identify the flight to which the baggage was to be sent, the position from which the aircraft was to leave and the time of the flight. The trays were dispatched to a waiting area where they circulated until an instruction was fed in to summon the baggage for a particular flight, whereupon the items would be automatically extracted from the waiting area and sent to the departure point. Local origin baggage was received at check-in desks. There was no detailed evidence as to how the check-in staff dealt with it, but such baggage was passed into the system. Transit baggage was taken to one of two areas, identified as V3 and HM respectively, where it was fed into the system at points known as coding stations. All baggage at the airport went through the automated system, with the exception of transit baggage when there was less than 45 minutes interval between flights. In that case, baggage might be taken from one aircraft to another without going through the system.

[27] There were seven coding stations in V3. One such station is shown in photographs in production 1053. The general practice was that baggage from an incoming flight was brought either to HM or to V3 in wagons or containers. On arrival, the baggage from a flight would be directed by an employee called the interline writer to one or more of the coding stations. The proper practice was that each coding station should not deal with baggage from more than one incoming flight at a time. Nor-

mally there were two employees at each coding station. One would lift the items of baggage from the wagon or container and place each item in a tray. The other would enter into the computer, in a coded form, the flight number and destination for the outgoing flight, taking the information from the tag attached to the item. There was evidence that from time to time there might be an additional employee at a coding station, who would assist in removing the baggage and placing it in trays, and that the details from the tag might be read out to the coder by the person putting the item into a tray. Rush tag items were dealt with in the same way as other items. Items which arrived at a coding station without a legible tag were sent to an error area to be dealt with there. Records were kept identifying the staff working at particular stations, the arrival times of aircraft, the arrival times of consignments of baggage at HM or V3, and the station or stations to which the baggage from a particular flight was sent. The computer itself retained a record of the items sent through the system so that it was possible, for a limited period, to identify all the items of baggage sent through the system to a particular flight. After some time, however, that information would be lost from the system. The baggage control system contained its own clock, and there was a tendency for the time recorded by that clock to diverge from real time. The baggage control clock was therefore reset at the start of each day, by reference either to the main computer clock or to the employee's watch. The divergence was progressive and by 4.00pm or 5.00pm the discrepancy might be as much as two or three minutes. Times entered in other records were obtained by the staff from the airport clock or from their own watches.

[28] PanAm had x-ray equipment at Frankfurt, which was used to x-ray interline baggage. The system was that baggage arriving at the departure gate for a PanAm flight would be separated into categories, according to the flight programme. In the case of PA103A, that meant that the loaders would separate baggage for London, baggage for New York, and interline baggage. The last category would be taken to the x-ray equipment and examined and returned to be loaded. The practice of PanAm at Frankfurt was to carry out a reconciliation between local origin passengers and baggage and online passengers and baggage, to ensure that every such passenger who had baggage on the flight was accounted for, but there was no attempt to reconcile interline passengers and their baggage. Reconciliation of interline passengers would have been difficult because the staff at the gate would not have any knowledge of an interline passenger until the passenger appeared to check in at the gate and receive a boarding card there. There was evidence from two witnesses, Roland O'Neill, the load master for PA103A, and Monika Diegmuller, a check-in supervisor, that there was a reconciliation of interline passengers and baggage, but there was overwhelming evidence to the contrary and their evidence on this point is not acceptable. The evidence that there was no reconciliation came from Herbert Leuniger, PanAm's director at Frankfurt, and Wolf Krommes, a duty station manager with PanAm. Further, in March 1988, Alan Berwick, the head of security for a wide area including the Middle East, after discussion with Martin Huebner, the security officer for PA at Frankfurt, sent a memorandum (production 1170) to Mr Sonesen, the company officer in New York to whom he reported, requesting a corporate decision on the question whether, in view of the existence of the x-ray facility, there should be any reconciliation. The

reply (production 1171) emphatically instructed that if baggage had been x-rayed, the aircraft should leave, even if the interline passenger to whom it belonged had not boarded, and that there should be no reconciliation. In early 1989, Mr O'Neill gave a statement to two FAA investigators in terms which implied that there was normally no reconciliation.

[29] The evidence of Joachim Koscha, who was one of the managers of the baggage system at Frankfurt in 1988, taken with production 1068, shows that flight KM180 reached its parking position at 1248 on 21 December 1988. Since it was not a PanAm flight it was unloaded by employees of the airport authority. According to the record, it was unloading between 1248 and 1300. Andreas Schreiner was in charge of monitoring the arrival of baggage at V3 on 21 December 1988. He made the following record on a document called the interline writer's sheet (production 1092):-

Flug no.	Pos.	ONB	Ank.	DW/Vw-Nr.	Anzahl	Wag.	Direkt Pos.	Von V3
KM180	141	1248	1301	146		1		

That bears to record one wagon of baggage from KM180, in position at 1248, arriving at V3 at 1301. Mr Schreiner's evidence was that coding would generally begin three to five minutes after the arrival of the baggage at V3. Mr Schreiner also said that luggage was always delivered from one flight only. Mr Schreiner and Mr Koscha further identified production 1061 as a work sheet completed by a coder to record baggage with which he dealt. The name of the coder in question was Koca, who was not called as a witness. The relevant part of production 1061 is as follows:-

Intestell	Flug Nr.	Kodierzeit Beginn	Ende	Cont. Nr.	Wag.	Kodierer Name
206	KM180	1304	1310	—	1	Koca

That record bears to show that one wagon of baggage from KM180 was coded at station 206 in V3 between 1304 and 1310. It was suggested that the figure for the completion of coding might be 1316, but Mr Schreiner preferred the reading 1310, which is more consistent with what can be seen on the document. There is also documentary evidence (prod1062) that the aircraft used for PA103A arrived from Vienna (as flight PA124) and was placed at position 44, from which it left for London at 1653.

[30] Mrs Bogomira Erac, a computer programmer employed at the airport, was on duty on 21 December 1988. She heard of the loss of PA103 during the evening of that day and realised that PA103A had departed during her period on duty. She was interested in the amount of baggage on the Frankfurt flight, and on the following morning she decided to take a printout of the information as to baggage held on the computer in case it should contain any useful information. She did not at once identify any such information, but retained the printout, which later was given to investigators. The printout is production 1060, and includes the following entry:-

Container no.	Flight no.	Counter no.	Time leave store	Time at gate
B8849	F1042	S0009 + Z1307 TO HS33 + Z1517		B044 + Z1523

The document itself contains no column headings, and those set out above are derived from the evidence showing how the printout is to be interpreted, by reference to the codes in operation at the time. The document therefore bears to record that an item coded at station 206 at 1307 was transferred and delivered to the appropriate gate to be loaded on board PA103A.

[31] The documentary evidence as a whole therefore clearly gives rise to the inference that an item which came in on KM180 was transferred to and left on PA103A. Evidence led in connection with KM180 established that there was no passenger who had an onward booking from Frankfurt to London or the United States and that all the passengers on KM180 retrieved all their checked-in baggage at their destinations. The Malta documentation for KM180 does not record that any unaccompanied baggage was carried. Defence counsel submitted that there was no evidence that baggage sent to the gate was actually loaded onto the flight, nor was there any count of the number of bags loaded. There was however evidence from Mr Kasteleiner that it could be taken from the documents that no baggage was left at the gate and it can be inferred that all items sent there were loaded. It follows that there is a plain inference from the documentary record that an unidentified and unaccompanied bag travelled on KM180 from Luqa airport to Frankfurt and there was loaded on PA103A.

****

[35] The evidence in regard to what happened at Frankfurt Airport, although of crucial importance, is only part of the evidence in the case and has to be considered along with all the other evidence before a conclusion can be reached as to where the primary suitcase originated and how it reached PA103. It can, however, be said at this stage that if the Frankfurt evidence is considered entirely by itself and without reference to any other evidence, none of the points made by the defence seems to us to cast doubt on the inference from the documents and other evidence that an unaccompanied bag from KM180 was transferred to and loaded onto PA103A.

[36] Luqa Airport was relatively small. The evidence did not disclose the exact number of check-in desks but the photographs in production 871 suggest that there were not very many. Behind the check-in desks there was a conveyor belt, and behind it there was a solid wall, separating the check-in area from the airside area. Behind the check-in desks there were three glass doors, again between the public area and airside, but these were kept locked. There were other doors between the airside and the open area, but at Luqa these were guarded by military personnel, who also dealt with security at other entrances to the airside area of the airport. The conveyor belt carried items of baggage along behind the check-in desks and passed through a small hatch into the airside baggage area. The hatch was also under observation by military

personnel and there were Customs officers present in the baggage area. The baggage area was restricted in size. As items of baggage passed along the conveyor belt they were checked for the presence of explosives by military personnel using a sniffer device. The device could detect the presence of many explosives but would not normally detect Semtex, although it might detect one of its constituents under certain circumstances. The only access from the check-in area to the sniffer area was through the hatch or through a separate guarded door.

[37] Air Malta acted as handling agents for all airlines flying out of Luqa. That meant that the check-in desks for all flights were manned by Air Malta staff. There were station managers and other staff of other airlines present at the airport. Some airlines insisted on the use of their own baggage tags, but Air Malta tags could be used for flights of other airlines, in certain circumstances. Whatever the purpose for which they were to be used, Air Malta tags were treated as a security item. They were kept in a store and supplies were issued to the check-in agents when a flight was due to start check-in. The same applied to interline tags. All remaining tags were returned to the supervisor after the check-in was completed.

[38] Luqa airport had a relatively elaborate security system. All items of baggage checked in were entered into the airport computer as well as being noted on the passenger's ticket. After the baggage had passed the sniffer check, it was placed on a trolley in the baggage area to wait until the flight was ready for loading. When the flight was ready, the baggage was taken out and loaded, and the head loader was required to count the items placed on board. The ramp dispatcher, the airport official on the tarmac responsible for the departure of the flight, was in touch by radiotelephone with the load control office. The load control had access to the computer and after the flight was closed would notify the ramp dispatcher of the number of items checked in. The ramp dispatcher would also be told by the head loader how many items had been loaded and if there was a discrepancy would take steps to resolve it. That might require a check of the ticket coupons, a check with one or more check-in agents or, in the last resort, a physical reconciliation by unloading the baggage and asking passengers to identify their own luggage. Interline bags would be included in the total known to load control, as would any rush items. It was suggested by the Crown that there might at one time have been a practice of allowing the aircraft to leave in spite of a discrepancy, if the discrepancy was less than five items, but the records referred to by the Crown did not bear out that this was a regular practice and the suggestion was firmly denied by the Air Malta and airport witnesses. In addition to the baggage reconciliation procedure, there was a triple count of the number of passengers boarding a departing flight, that is there was a count of the boarding cards, a count by immigration officers of the number of immigration cards handed in, and a head count by the crew. On the face of them, these arrangements seem to make it extremely difficult for an unaccompanied and unidentified bag to be shipped on a flight out of Luqa. It was suggested that there were occasions, particularly when an LAA flight was being checked in, when conditions at the check-in desks were crowded and chaotic because a great deal of miscellaneous and unusual baggage was brought to the desks anbecause the queues were not orderly. It was therefore suggested that on

such an occasion a bag might have been slipped onto the conveyor belt behind the desks without anyone noticing. Again, evidence was led that on occasions airline representatives, such as the second accused, would assist favoured passengers by helping them to obtain special treatment at the check-in and immigration desks and placing baggage on the conveyor. Evidence to that effect was given by Dennis Burke and Nicholas Ciarlo who worked as travel agents at the airport but none of the evidence went further than suggesting that a case might have been placed on the conveyor belt, from where it would have gone to the explosives check and the baggage area, but not escaping the baggage reconciliation system. The evidence of the responsible officials at the airport, particularly Wilfred Borg, the Air Malta general manager for ground operations at the time, was that it was impossible or highly unlikely that a bag could be introduced undetected at the check-in desks or in the baggage area, or by approaching the loaders, in view of the restricted areas in which the operations proceeded and the presence of Air Malta, Customs and military personnel. Mr Borg conceded that it might not be impossible that a bag could be introduced undetected but said that whether it was probable was another matter.

[39] As regards the flight itself, the check-in for KM180 opened at 0815 and closed at 0915. There were two other flight check-ins open during that period or part of it. Flight KM220 was checking in between 0835 and 0930 and an LAA flight, LN147, was checking in between 0850 and 0950. The records relating to KM180 on 21 December 1988 show no discrepancy in respect of baggage. The flight log (production 930) shows that fifty-five items of baggage were loaded, corresponding to fifty-five on the load plan. There was a good deal of evidence led in relation to the number of items noted on the ticket counterfoils for the flight, and especially in regard to the number of items checked in by a German television crew who travelled on the flight. It does not seem to us to be necessary to examine that evidence in detail. A discrepancy might have masked the presence of an additional item, but the evidence is inconclusive as to whether or not there was any discrepancy and in any event it is difficult to suppose that a person launching a bomb into the interline system would rely on such a chance happening. If therefore the unaccompanied bag was launched from Luqa, the method by which that was done is not established, and the Crown accepted that they could not point to any specific route by which the primary suitcase could have been loaded. Counsel for the defence pointed out that neither the head loader nor the other members of the loading crew were called to give evidence, and submitted that, in their absence, the Crown could not ask the court to draw any inference adverse to them. The absence of any explanation of the method by which the primary suitcase might have been placed on board KM180 is a major difficulty for the Crown case, and one which has to be considered along with the rest of the circumstantial evidence in the case.

[40] We turn now to consider what evidence there is to establish any involvement on the part of either or both of the accused.

[41] In relation to the first accused, there are three important witnesses, Abdul Majid, Edwin Bollier and Tony Gauci.

[42] Abdul Majid in 1984 joined the Jamahariya Security Organisation ("JSO"), later named the External Security Organisation. His initial employment was in the vehicle maintenance department for about eighteen months. In December 1985 he was appointed as assistant to the station manager of LAA at Luqa airport. This post was one which was normally filled by a member of the JSO. He gave evidence about the organisation of the JSO in 1985. In particular he said that the director of the central security section was Ezzadin Hinshiri, the head of the operations section was Said Rashid, the head of special operations in the operations department was Nassr Ashur, and the head of the airline security section was the first accused until January 1987 when he moved to the strategic studies institute. The second accused was the station manager for LAA at Luqa from 1985 until about October 1988. While Abdul Majid was only a junior member of the JSO, we are prepared to accept that he was aware of the hierarchy and that his evidence on these matters can be accepted. ************

[43] *************** Putting the matter shortly, we are unable to accept Abdul Majid as a credible and reliable witness on any matter except his description of the organisation of the JSO and the personnel involved there.

[44]   The next important issue is that relating to MST-13 timers. The evidence relating to this came essentially from Edwin Bollier, Erwin Meister, Ulrich Lumpert and those who supplied the circuit board components of the timers from Thuring AG, Zurich. MEBO AG was formed in the early 1970s by Edwin Bollier and Erwin Meister. In 1985 it had its offices in the Novapark Hotel (now the Continental Hotel) in Zurich. By then it had for some years supplied electrical, electronic and surveillance equipment. At that time, according to Mr Bollier, its principal customer was the Libyan Government and in particular the Libyan military security, and in connection with that business he made fairly frequent visits to Libya. Mr Lumpert was employed by the company as an engineer and in that capacity he was involved in the design and production of such equipment.

[45]   We have assessed carefully the evidence of these three witnesses about the activities of MEBO, and in particular their evidence relating to the MST-13 timers which the company made. All three, and notably Mr Bollier, were shown to be unreliable witnesses.
****

[46] ************* It was established, and Mr Meister was forced to accept, that the Olympus timer was incapable of showing a date. Moreover, the evidence of both witnesses about what they claimed to have seen and the circumstances in which they claimed to have made the discovery was so inconsistent that we are wholly unable to accept any of it.

****

[49] We do however accept certain parts of Mr Bollier's evidence despite finding him at times an untruthful and at other times an unreliable witness. We have done so

when his evidence has not been challenged and appears to have been accepted, or where it is supported from some other acceptable source. We accept, for example, that in or about July 1985 on a visit to Tripoli, Mr Bollier received a request for electronic timers from Said Rashid or Ezzadin Hinshiri and that he had had military business dealings in relation to the Libyan Government with Ezzadin Hinshiri since the early 1980s. The potential order was for a large number of such timers. Mr Lumpert was told of the requirements by Mr Bollier and proceeded to develop two prototypes. There is a dispute in the evidence between Mr Bollier and Mr Meister on the one hand and Mr Lumpert on the other about the colour of the circuit boards in these prototype timers. Mr Bollier said they were brown, Mr Meister thought they were grey or brown, whereas Mr Lumpert said that they were manufactured from the green coloured circuit boards supplied by Thuring. What we do however accept is that later in the summer of 1985 the two prototypes were delivered by Mr Bollier to the Stasi in East Berlin, whatever be the colour of their circuit boards. This is consistent with the evidence of Mr Wenzel who at the material time was a major in the Stasi and with whom Mr Bollier then dealt. Despite this evidence we cannot, however, exclude absolutely the possibility that more than two MST-13 timers were supplied by MEBO to the Stasi, although there is no positive evidence that they were, nor any reasons why they should have been. Similarly, we cannot exclude the possibility that other MST-13 timers may have been made by MEBO and supplied to other parties, but there is no positive evidence that they were. Equally, despite the evidence of Mr Wenzel that after the fall of the Berlin wall he had destroyed all timers supplied to the Stasi, we are unable to exclude the possibility that any MST-13 timers in the hands of the Stasi left their possession, although there is no positive evidence that they did and in particular that they were supplied to the PFLP-GC.

[50] The initial order placed with Thuring was for twenty circuit boards, solder masked on one side only, i.e. single sided. In fact Thuring supplied twenty-four such boards. In October 1985 MEBO placed a further order with Thuring for circuit boards but it was specified that they should be solder masked on both sides, i.e. double sided. Thirty-five such boards were ordered, but Thuring supplied only thirty-four. When the Scottish police visited MEBO's premises in May 1991, CI Williamson received from Mr Bollier eleven circuit boards, having been shown twelve. Earlier, on 15 November 1990, following the interview by a Swiss Magistrate of Mr Bollier and Mr Meister, CI Williamson also took possession of two sample MST-13 timers. It is clear from this, therefore, that at least twelve of the circuit boards ordered from Thuring were not used in the manufacture of MST-13 timers. Of the number which CI Williamson took into his possession, four were single sided circuit boards. Of the circuit boards in the sample MST-13 timers recovered by CI Williamson, one was single sided and the other double sided. The MST-13 timer which the US authorities obtained from the Togo Government in September or October 1986 at Lomé (to which reference will later be made) also had a double sided circuit board. It follows that some of the circuit boards of these timers were single sided and some were double sided, and also that a number of the single sided circuit boards supplied by Thuring in August 1985 were not used. Mr Bollier therefore may well have been correct when he said that the Libyan order was met with the supply of timers which had circuit

boards of both types. We also accept Mr Bollier's evidence that he supplied the twenty samples to Libya in three batches. In 1985 he himself delivered five on a visit to Tripoli. In the same year he delivered another five to the Libyan Embassy in East Berlin. In 1986 he delivered the remaining ten personally in Tripoli.

****

[55] The third important witness is Mr Gauci. We have already referred to his evidence in connection with the sale of clothing. Mr Gauci picked out the first accused at an identification parade on 13 August 1999, using the words as written in the parade report "Not exactly the man I saw in the shop. Ten years ago I saw him, but the man who look a little bit like exactly is the number 5". Number 5 in the parade was the first accused. He also identified him in Court, saying "He is the man on this side. He resembles him a lot". These identifications were criticised *inter alia* on the ground that photographs of the accused have featured many times over the years in the media and accordingly purported identifications more than ten years after the event are of little if any value. Before assessing the quality and value of these identifications it is important to look at the history.

[56] In his evidence in chief, Mr Gauci said that the date of purchase must have been about a fortnight before Christmas. He was asked if he could be more specific under reference to the street Christmas decorations. Initially he said "I wouldn't know exactly, but I have never really noticed these things, but I remember, yes, there were Christmas lights. They were on already. I'm sure. I can't say exactly". In a later answer when it had been put to him that he had earlier said that the sale was before the Christmas decorations went up, he said "I don't know. I'm not sure what I told them exactly about this. I believe they were putting up the lights, though, in those times." He could not say what day of the week it was. He was alone in the shop because his brother was at home watching football on television. When asked about the weather he said "When he came by the first time, it wasn't raining but then it started dripping. Not very — it was not raining heavily. It was simply dripping..." As we have previously noted, he said the purchaser was a Libyan. He was wearing a blue suit. When asked about the build of the purchaser, he said "I'm not an expert on these things. I think he was below six feet....He wasn't small. He was a normal stature. He had ordered a 16½ shirt". When asked about age he said "I said before, below six – under sixty. I don't have experience on height and age." He also said the purchaser had dark coloured skin. On 13 September he went to the police station where he assisted in the compilation of a photofit (production 430.1) and an artist's impression (production 427.1). He described the result of both as being 'very close'.

[57] In cross-examination he had put to him a number of statements he had made to the police. He was first interviewed by the police on 1 September 1989. On that date, in addition to giving the police information about the clothing, he also gave information about the circumstances of the sale, the date of the sale, and the description of the purchaser. In the statement noted by DCI Bell on that date, Mr Gauci said that he had been working alone in the shop between 6.30pm and 7.00pm when the pur-

chaser came in. The description of the purchaser as given to DCI Bell was that he was six feet or more in height. He had a big chest and a large head. He was well built but was not fat or with a big stomach. His hair was very black. He was clean-shaven with no facial hair and had dark coloured skin. His overall appearance was smart. He bought an umbrella and put it up when he left the shop because it was raining. Mr Gauci said that he could not remember the day of the week although he thought it was a weekday. In a further statement on 13 September he said that the man was about 50 years of age.

[58] On 14 September 1989 Mr Gauci was taken to police headquarters at Floriana, Malta, where he was interviewed by DCI Bell and Inspector Scicluna of the Maltese police. They took a statement from him and showed him nineteen photographs on two cards. Mr Gauci identified a photograph of a man in one of the cards. He said that he was similar to the man who had bought the clothing but the man in the photograph he identified was too young to be the man who had bought the clothing. If he was older by about twenty years he would have looked like the man who bought the clothing. He signed the front of the photograph of the man whom he identified as similar. He said in his statement that the photograph looked like the man's features so far as the eyes, nose, mouth and shape of face were concerned. The hair of the customer was similar but shorter than that of the man in the photograph. DCI Bell revealed that the person whom Mr Gauci had identified was someone whom the Maltese Security Branch considered to be similar to the artist and photo-fit impressions which had been composed as a result of the description given by Mr Gauci. The man was later identified as one Mohammed Salem.

[59] On 26 September 1989 Mr Gauci again attended at police headquarters in Malta where he was interviewed by the same two police officers. He was then shown more photographs. He said that he did not see the man to whom he sold the clothing, but he pointed out one photograph of a man who had the shairstyle. He said that this was not the man he sold the clothing to as the man in the photograph was too young. The person he pointed out, according to the evidence of DCI Bell, was a person called Shukra whose photograph was included at the suggestion of the BKA, the German police force, who suggested that Shukra might be similar to the person whom Mr Gauci had already described.

[60] On 31 August 1990 Mr Gauci gave a further statement to DCI Bell and Inspector Scicluna at police headquarters at Floriana. He was shown a card containing twelve photographs. He examined these photographs and said that he could not see the photograph of the man who had purchased the clothing, and he told DCI Bell that the man's photograph was not present. He pointed out one of the photographs of a man who was similar in the shape of the face and style of hair but it was not, he said, the photograph of the man whom he had described. He informed DCI Bell that three other photographs he was shown were photographs of men of the correct age of the man he had described. DCI Bell then opened another set of photographs, twelve in number. Mr Gauci examined each of these but could not see the photograph of the man who had purchased the clothing. DCI Bell gave evidence that in the first series

there was included a photograph of a man Marzouk and in the second series a man named Saber. He could not however say which photographs represented either person.

[61] On 10 September 1990 Mr Gauci again attended at police headquarters. He was shown thirty-nine photographs on that occasion which were contained in an album. He however made no identification of anyone from these photographs which included a photograph of Abo Talb. Mr Gauci had been shown on 6 December 1989 a selection of photographs which included a photograph of Abo Talb, but he made no identification of anyone from these photographs. At about the end of 1989 or the beginning of 1990 his brother showed him an article in a newspaper about the Lockerbie disaster. As he recalled, there were photographs of two people in the article. Across the photograph of the wreckage of Pan Am 103 there was printed the word "Bomber". In the top right corner of the article there was a photograph of a man with the word "Bomber" also across it. Mr Gauci thought that one of the photographs showed the man who had bought the articles from him. When the Advocate Depute put to Mr Gauci in evidence at the trial that the man in the photograph looked similar to the man who had bought the clothes, Mr Gauci replied that it resembled him and he explained that the man's face and hair resembled the person who had bought the clothes from him. The person whom he identified in that way was Abo Talb. By the time he gave his statement on 10 September 1990 Mr Gauci had been shown many photographs but he said in that statement that he had never seen a photograph of the man who had bought the clothing.

[62] On 15 February 1991 Mr Gauci again attended at police headquarters. He was asked to look at a number of photographs and a card of twelve photographs was put before him. He said: "The first impression I had was that all the photographs were of men younger than the man who bought the clothing. I told Mr Bell this. I was asked to look at all the photographs carefully and to try and allow for any age difference. I then pointed out one of the photographs." He said of the photograph of the person he had pointed out: "Number 8 is similar to the man who bought the clothing. The hair is perhaps a bit long. The eyebrows are the same. The nose is the same. And his chin and shape of face are the same. The man in the photograph number 8 is in my opinion in his 30 years. He would perhaps have to look about 10 years or more older, and he would look like the man who bought the clothes. It's been a long time now, and I can only say that this photograph 8 resembles the man who bought the clothing, but it is younger." He went on further to say: "I can only say that of all the photographs I have been shown, this photograph number 8 is the only one really similar to the man who bought the clothing, if he was a bit older, other than the one my brother showed me." He was asked by DCI Bell if what he said was true and that this photograph was the only one really similar to the man who bought the clothing if he was a bit older, other than the one his brother had shown him, and he said: "Of course. He didn't have such long hair, either. His hair wasn't so large." DCI Bell later gave evidence that the person shown in photograph 8 was the first accused, being apparently the same as the photograph in the first accused's 1986 passport. He also said that before showing Mr Gauci the card of photographs he had all the other

photographs dulled down to the same level of brightness as the first accused's photograph. He said that he did that simply for fairness because the rest of the photographs were brighter and sharper than that of the first accused and he wanted them all to look the same. Counsel for the first accused submitted that DCI Bell's attempts to make the quality of all the photographs similar had failed, but in our view this criticism has no validity.

[63] Finally, so far as police interviews were concerned, Mr Gauci was asked about a visit he made to Inspector Scicluna towards the end of 1998 or the beginning of 1999 after another shopkeeper showed him a magazine containing an article about the Lockerbie disaster. Towards the bottom of the page in the article there was a photograph in the centre of a man wearing glasses. Mr Gauci thought that that man looked like the man who had bought the clothes from him but his hair was much shorter and he didn't wear glasses. He showed the photograph in the article to Inspector Scicluna and, as Mr Gauci recalled it, he said "Well now I said 'This chap looks like the man who bought articles from me.' Something like that I told him." He added that the hair of the man who bought from him was much shorter than that shown in the photograph and he was without glasses. The photograph was a photograph of the first accused.

[64] In cross-examination Mr Gauci was referred to a statement which he had given to DCI Bell on 14 September 1989. In that statement he said that the purchase of the clothing was made on a week day when he was alone in the shop. His brother Paul Gauci did not work in the shop on that particular afternoon because he had gone home to watch a football match on television. It was agreed by Joint Minute that whichever football match or matches Paul Gauci had watched would have been broadcast by Italian Radio Television either on 23 November 1988 or 7 December 1988. Mr Gauci had also said in that statement that the purchaser walked out of the shop with the umbrella which he had purchased and that he had opened up the umbrella as it was raining. In his evidence he agreed that he had said this because it was raining at the time. When the man returned, the umbrella was down because it had almost stopped raining. There were just a few drops coming down. In a later statement he said that it had almost stopped raining when the man came back and there were just a few drops still coming down. It wasn't raining, he said in evidence, it was just drizzling. In a statement dated 10 September 1990 which was put to him in cross-examination he said that just before the man left the shop there was a light shower of rain just beginning. As the man left the shop he opened up the umbrella which he had just purchased. "There was very little rain on the ground, no running water, just damp." He was also asked in cross-examination what he meant when he used the word "midweek" and he responded by saying that he meant a Wednesday. It was put to him that midweek meant a day which was separate from the weekend, in other words that the shop would be open the day before and the day after. To that Mr Gauci said "That's it. Exactly. Tuesday and Thursday." But he then went on to say that for him midweek was Wednesday. It was not put to him that Thursday 8 December 1988 was a pubholiday, it being the feast of the Immaculate Conception on that day. That evidence was given on Day 76 by Major Mifsud in the course of evidence

led for the first accused. We are satisfied that when Mr Gauci was asked whether the shop would be open the day before and the day after he was being asked what he meant by the word "midweek", and not whether the day after the purchase of the clothing was made in his shop, the shop was open for business.

[65] Major Mifsud was between 1979 and 1988 the Chief Meteorologist at the Meteorological Office at Luqa Airport. He was shown the meteorological records kept by his department for the two periods, 7/8 December 1988 and 23/24 November 1988. He said that on 7 December 1988 at Luqa there was a trace of rain which fell at 9.00am but apart from that no rain was recorded later in the day. Sliema is about five kilometres from Luqa. When he was asked whether rain might have fallen at Sliema between 6.00pm. and 7.00pm in the evening of 7 December 1988, he explained that although there was cloud cover at the time he would say "that 90% was no rain" but there was however always the possibility that there could be some drops of rain, "about 10% probability, in other places." He thought a few drops of rain might have fallen but he wouldn't think that the ground would have been made damp. To wet the ground the rain had to last for quite some time. The position so far as 23 November 1988 was concerned was different. At Luqa there was light intermittent rain on that day from noon onwards which by 1800 hours GMT had produced 0.6 of a millimetre of rain. He thought that the situation in the Sliema area would have been very much the same.

[66] Counsel for the first accused drew our attention to evidence which Mr Gauci gave that according to an invoice which he received, dated 25 November 1988, he purchased eight pairs of pyjamas about that time. Pyjamas sold well in winter and he used to buy stock "when it finished". According to a previous invoice dated 31 October 1988 he had at that time bought sixteen pairs. Since the purchaser of the clothing had bought two pairs of pyjamas and Mr Gauci had renewed his stock around 25 November 1988, counsel asked us to infer that the purchase of the two pairs must have been made on 23 November 1988. We are unable to draw this inference. In the first place it was not put to Mr Gauci in evidence that this may have been the sequence of events. Secondly, Mr Gauci was not asked what the state of his stock of pyjamas was on or about 7 December 1988.

[67] In assessing Mr Gauci's evidence we should first deal with a suggestion made in the submissions for the first accused that his demeanour was unsatisfactory – reluctant to look the cross examiner in the eye, a strange and lonely man, and enjoying the attention he was getting. We have to say we find no substance in any of these criticisms. We are not clear on what basis it was said that he was strange and lonely, and as far as enjoying attention is concerned, he made it clear that his co-operation with the investigation was a source of some friction within his family. The clear impression that we formed was that he was in the first place entirely credible, that is to say doing his best to tell the truth to the best of his recollection, and indeed no suggestion was made to the contrary. That of course is not an end of the matter, as even the most credible of witnesses may be unreliable or plainly wrong. We are satisfied that on two matters he was entirely reliable, namely the list of clothing that he sold and the fact

that the purchaser was a Libyan. On the matter of identification of the first accused, there are undoubtedly problems. We are satisfied with Mr Gauci's recollection, which he has maintained throughout, that his brother was watching football on the material date, and that narrows the field to 23 November or 7 December. There is no doubt that the weather on 23 November would be wholly consistent with a light shower between 6.30pm and 7.00pm. The possibility that there was a brief light shower on 7 December is not however ruled out by the evidence of Major Mifsud. It is perhaps unfortunate that Mr Gauci was never asked if he had any recollection of the weather at any other time on that day, as evidence that this was the first rain of the day would have tended to favour 7 December over 23 November. While Major Mifsud's evidence was clear about the position at Luqa, he did not rule out the possibility of a light shower at Sliema. Mr Gauci's recollection of the weather was that "it started dripping – not raining heavily" or that there was a "drizzle", and it only appeared to last for the time that the purchaser was away from the shop to get a taxi, and the taxi rank was not far away. The position about the Christmas decorations was unclear, but it would seem consistent with Mr Gauci's rather confused recollection that the purchase was about the time when the decorations would be going up, which in turn would be consistent with his recollection in evidence that it was about two weeks before Christmas. We are unimpressed by the suggestion that because Thursday 8 December was a public holiday, Mr Gauci should have been able to fix the date by reference to that. Even if there was some validity in that suggestion, it loses any value when it was never put to him for his comments. Having carefully considered all the factors relating to this aspect, we have reached the conclusion that the date of purchase was Wednesday 7December.

[68] Mr Gauci's initial description to DCI Bell would not in a number of respects fit the first accused. At the identification parade the first accused's height was measured at 5'8". His age in December 1988 was 36. Mr Gauci said that he did not have experience of height or age, but even so it has to be accepted that there was a substantial discrepancy. Counsel for the first accused also pointed out that when the witness having pointed to the first accused in court, and asked which of the two accused he was referring to, said "Not the dark one, the other one", and the first accused was the other one. When however he first saw a photograph of the first accused in a montage of twelve, he picked him out in the terms we have indicated above.

[69] What did appear to us to be clear was that Mr Gauci applied his mind carefully to the problem of identification whenever he was shown photographs, and did not just pick someone out at random. Unlike many witnesses who express confidence in their identification when there is little justification for it, he was always careful to express any reservations he had and gave reasons why he thought that there was a resemblance. There are situations where a careful witness who will not commit himself beyond saying that there is a close resemblance can be regarded as more reliable and convincing in his identification than a witness who maintains that his identification is 100% certain. From his general demeanour and his approach to the difficult problem of identification, we formed the view that when he picked out the first accused at the identification parade and in Court, he was doing so not just because it

was comparatively easy to do so but because he genuinely felt that he was correct in picking him out as having a close resemblance to the purchaser, and we did regard him as a careful witness who would not commit himself to an absolutely positive identification when a substantial period had elapsed. We accept of course that he never made what could be described as an absolutely positive identification, but having regard to the lapse of time it would have been surprising if he had been able to do so. We have also not overlooked the difficulties in relation to his description of height and age. We are nevertheless satisfied that his identification so far as it went of the first accused as the purchaser was reliable and should be treated as a highly important element in this case. We should add that we have not made any attempt to compare for ourselves any resemblance between the first accused's passport photograph and tidentikit or artist's impression, nor with the first accused's appearance in the video recordings of his interview with Pierre Salinger in November 1991.

****

[82] From the evidence which we have discussed so far, we are satisfied that it has been proved that the primary suitcase containing the explosive device was dispatched from Malta, passed through Frankfurt and was loaded onto PA103 at Heathrow. It is, as we have said, clear that with one exception the clothing in the primary suitcase was the clothing purchased in Mr Gauci's shop on 7 December 1988. The purchaser was, on Mr Gauci's evidence, a Libyan. The trigger for the explosion was an MST-13 timer of the single solder mask variety. A substantial quantity of such timers had been supplied to Libya. We cannot say that it is impossible that the clothing might have been taken from Malta, united somewhere with a timer from some source other than Libya and introduced into the airline baggage system at Frankfurt or Heathrow. When, however, the evidence regarding the clothing, the purchaser and the timer is taken with the evidence that an unaccompanied bag was taken from KM180 to PA103A, the inference that that was the primary suitcase becomes, in our view, irresistible. As we have also said, the absence of an explanation as to how the suitcase was taken into the system at Luqa is a major difficulty for the Crown case but after taking full account of that difficulty, we remain of the view that the primary suitcase began its journey at Luqa. The clear inference which we draw from this evidence is that the conception, planning and execution of the plot which led to the planting of the explosive device was of Libyan origin. While no doubt organisations such as the PFLP-GC and the PPSF were also engaged in terrorist activities during the same period, we are satisfied that there was no evidence from which we could infer that they were involved in this particular act of terrorism, and the evidence relating to their activities does not create a reasonable doubt in our minds about the Libyan origin of this crime.

[83] In that context we turn to consider the evidence which could be regarded as implicating either or both of the accus, bearing in mind that the evidence against each of them has to be considered separately, and that before either could be convicted we would have to be satisfied beyond reasonable doubt as to his guilt and that evidence from a single source would be insufficient.

[84] We deal first with the second accused. The principal piece of evidence against him comes from two entries in his 1988 diary. This was recovered in April 1991 from the offices of Medtours, a company which had been set up by the second accused and Mr Vassallo. At the back of the diary there were two pages of numbered notes. The fourteenth item on one page is translated as "Take/collect tags from the airport (Abdulbaset/Abdussalam)". The word 'tags' was written in English, the remainder in Arabic. On the diary page for 15 December there was an entry, preceded by an asterisk, "Take taggs from Air Malta", and at the end of that entry in a different coloured ink "OK". Again the word 'taggs' (sic) was in English. The Crown maintained that the inference to be drawn from these entries was that the second accused had obtained Air Malta interline tags for the first accused, and that as an airline employee he must have known that the only purpose for which they would be required was to enable an unaccompanied bag to be placed on an aircraft. From another entry on 15 December (translated as "Abdel-baset arriving from Zurich") it appears that the second accused expected the first accused to pass through Malta on that day. In fact the first accused passed through on 17 December and missed seeing the second accused. In his interview with Mr Salinger in November 1991, the second accused said that he had been informed by his partner Mr Vassallo that the first accused had spoken to him and asked him to tell the second accused that he wanted to commission him with something. On 18 December the second accused travelled to Tripoli. He returned on 20 December on the same flight as the first accused. The Crown maintained that the inference to be drawn from this was that on that date the first accused was bringing component parts of the explosive device into Malta, and required the company of the second accused to carry the suitcase through Customs as the second accused was well known to the customs officers who would be unlikely to stop him and search the case. This would be consistent with the evidence of Abdul Majid. Finally the Crown maintained that in order for the suitcase to get past the security checks at Luqa on 21 December and find its way on board KM180, someone would have to organise this who was very well acquainted with the security controls at Luqa and would know how these controls could be circumvented. As someone who had been a station manager for some years, the second accused was ideally fitted for this role. Further, there was a telephone call recorded from the Holiday Inn, where the first accused was staying, to the number of the second accused's flat at 7.11am on 21 December. The Crown argued that this could be inferred to be a call arranging for the second accused to give the first accused a lift to the airport, and also it could be inferred that the second accused was at the airport from the fact that the first accused received special treatment both at check-in and at immigration control before departing on the LN147 flight to Tripoli.

[85] There is no doubt that the second accused did make the entries in the diary to which we have referred. In the context of the explosive device being placed on KM180 at Luqa in a suitcase which must have had attached to it an interline tag to enable it to pass eventually on to PA103, these entries can easily be seen to have a sinister connotation, particularly in the complete absence of any form of explanation. Counsel for the second accused argued that even if it be accepted that the second accused did obtain tags and did supply them to the first accused, it would be going too far to infer

that he was necessarily aware that they were to be used for the purpose of blowing up an aircraft, bearing in mind that the Crown no longer suggest that the second accused was a member of the Libyan Intelligence Service. Had it been necessary to resolve this matter, we would have found it a difficult problem. For the reasons we are about to explain however we do not find it necessary to do so. The Crown attach significance to the visit by the second accused to Tripoli on 18 December 1988 and his return two days later in the company of the first accused. As we have indicated, we cannot accept the evidence of Abdul Majid that he saw the two accused arriving with a suitcase. It follows that there is no evidence that either of them had any luggage, let alone a brown Samsonite suitcase. Whatever else may have been the purpose of the second accused going to Tripoli, it is unlikely that his visit was to hand over tags, as this could easily have been done in Malta. We do not think it proper to draw the inference that the second accused went to Tripoli for the purpose, as the Crown suggested, of escorting the first accused through Customs at Luqa. There is no real foundation for this supposition, and we would regard it as speculation rather than inference. The position on this aspect therefore is that the purpose of the visit by the second accused to Tripoli is simply unknown, and while there may be a substantial element of suspicion, it cannot be elevated beyond the realm of suspicion. The Crown may be well founded in saying that the second accused would be aware of the security arrangements at Luqa, and therefore might have been aware of some way in which these arrangements could be circumvented. The Crown however go further and say that it was the second accused "who was in a position to and did render the final assistance in terms of introduction of the bag by whatever means". There is no evidence in our opinion which can be used to justify this proposition and therefore at best it must be in the realm of speculation. Furthermore, there is the formidable objection that there is no evidence at all to suggest that the second accused was even at Luqa airport on 21 December. There were a number of witnesses who were there that day who knew the second accused well, such as Abdul Majid and Anna Attard, and they were not even asked about the second accused's presence. The Crown suggestion that the brief telephone call to the second accused's flat on the morning of 21 December can by a series of inferences lead to the conclusion that he was at the airport is in our opinion wholly speculative. While therefore there may well be a sinister inference to be drawn from the diary entries, we have come to the conclusion that there is insufficient other acceptable evidence to support or confirm such an inference, in particular an inference that the second accused was aware that any assistance he was giving to the first accused was in connection with a plan to destroy an aircraft by the planting of an explosive device. There is therefore in our opinion insufficient corroboration for any adverse inference that might be drawn from the diary entries. In these circumstances the second accused falls to be acquitted.

[86] We now turn to the case against the first accused. We should make it clear at the outset that the entries in the second accused's diary can form no part of any case against the first accused. The entries fall to be treated as equivalent to a statement made by a co-accused outwith the presence of the first accused. If both accused had been proved by other evidence to have been acting in concert in the commission of the crime libelled, then these entries could perhaps have been used as general evi-

dence in the case as against any person proved to have been acting in concert. As we are of opinion however that it has not been proved that the second accused was a party to this crime, it follows that the normal rule must apply and the entries cannot be used against the first accused. We therefore put that matter entirely out of our minds.

[87] On 15 June 1987 the first accused was issued with a passport with an expiry date of 14 June 1991 by the Libyan passport authority at the request of the ESO who supplied the details to be included. The name on the passport was Ahmed Khalifa Abdusamad. Such a passport was known as a coded passport. There was no evidence as to why this passport was issued to him. It was used by the first accused on a visit to Nigeria in August 1987, returning to Tripoli via Zurich and Malta, travelling at least between Zurich and Tripoli on the same flights as Nassr Ashur who was also travelling on a coded passport. It was also used during 1987 for visits to Ethiopia, Saudi Arabia and Cyprus. The only use of this passport in 1988 was for an overnight visit to Malta on 20/21 December, and it was never used again. On that visit he arrived in Malta on flight KM231 about 5.30pm. He stayed overnight in the Holiday Inn, Sliema, using the name Abdusamad. He left on 21 December on flight LN147, scheduled to leave at 10.20am. The first accused travelled on his own passport in his own name on a number of occasions in 1988, particularly to Malta on 7 December where he stayed until 9 December when he departed for Prague, returning to Tripoli via Zurich and Malta on 16/17 December.

[88] A major factor in the case against the first accused is the identification evidence of Mr Gauci. For the reasons we have already given, we accept the reliability of Mr Gauci on this matter, while recognising that this is not an unequivocal identification. From his evidence it could be inferred that the first accused was the person who bought the clothing which surrounded the explosive device. We have already accepted that the date of purchase of the clothing was 7 December 1988, and on that day the first accused arrived in Malta where he stayed until 9 December. He was staying at the Holiday Inn, Sliema, which is close to Mary's House. If he was the purchaser of this miscellaneous collection of garments, it is not difficult to infer that he must have been aware of the purpose for which they were being bought. We accept the evidence that he was a member of the JSO, occupying posts of fairly high rank. One of these posts was head of airline security, from which it could be inferred that he would be aware at least in general terms of the nature of security precautions at airports from or to which LAA operated. He also appears to have been involved in military procurement. He was involved with Mr Bollier, albeit not specifically in connection with MST timers, and had along with Badri Hassan formed a company which leased premises from MEBO and intended to do business with MEBO. In his interview with Mr Salinger he denied any connection with MEBO, but we do not accept his denial. On 20 December 1988 he entered Malta using his passport in the name of Abdusamad. There is no apparent reason for this visit, so far as the evidence discloses. All that was revealed by acceptable evidence was that the first accused and the second accused together paid a brief visit to the house of Mr Vassallo at some time in the evening, and that the first accused made or attempted to make a phone call to

the second accused at 7.11am the following morning. It is possible to infer that this visit under a false name the night before the explosive device was planted at Luqa, followed by his departure for Tripoli the following morning at or about the time the device must have been planted, was a visit connected with the planting of the device. Had there been any innocent explanation for this visit, obviously this inference could not be drawn. The only explanation that appeared in the evidence was contained in his interview with Mr Salinger, when he denied visiting Malta at that time and denied using the name Abdusamad or having had a passport in that name. Again, we do not accept his denial.

[89] We are aware that in relation to certain aspects of the case there are a number of uncertainties and qualifications. We are also aware that there is a danger that by selecting parts of the evidence which seem to fit together and ignoring parts which might not fit, it is possible to read into a mass of conflicting evidence a pattern or conclusion which is not really justified. However, having considered the whole evidence in the case, including the uncertainties and qualifications, and the submissions of counsel, we are satisfied that the evidence as to the purchase of clothing in Malta, the presence of that clothing in the primary suitcase, the transmission of an item of baggage from Malta to London, the identification of the first accused (albeit not absolute), his movements under a false name at or around the material time, and the other background circumstances such as his association with Mr Bollier and with members of the JSO or Libyan military who purchased MST-13 timers, does fit together to form a real and convincing pattern. There is nothing in the evidence which leaves us with any reasonable doubt as to the guilt of the first accused, and accordingly we find him guilty of the remaining charge in the Indictment as amended.

[90] The verdicts returned were by a unanimous decision of the three judges of the Court.

DOCUMENT No. 10A

UNITED STATES DISTRICT COURT
SOUTHERN DISTRICT OF NEW YORK
UNITED STATES OF AMERICA

v.

USAMA BIN LADEN, et al.,

New York, N.Y.

May 29, 2001 9:15 a.m.

Before:

HON. LEONARD B. SAND,

District Judge

(Edited Transcript)

...THE CLERK: Madam Forelady, has the jury reached a verdict?

THE FOREPERSON: Yes, we have.

THE CLERK: On Count 1, how do you find as to the defendant Wadih El Hage?

THE FOREPERSON: On Count 1, we find the defendant Wadih El Hage guilty.

THE CLERK: How do you find as to the defendant Mohamed Sadeek Odeh?

THE FOREPERSON: We find Mohamed Sadeek Odeh guilty.

THE CLERK: How do you find as to Mohamed Rashed Daoud al-'Owhali?

THE FOREPERSON: We find Mohamed Rashed Daoud al-'Owhali guilty.

THE CLERK: How do you find as to the defendant Khalfan Khamis Mohamed?

THE FOREPERSON: Khalfan Khamis Mohamed guilty.

THE CLERK: On Count 2, how do you find as to the defendant Wadih El Hage?

THE FOREPERSON: Wadih El Hage guilty.

THE CLERK: How do you find as to the defendant Mohamed Sadeek Odeh?

THE FOREPERSON: Mohamed Sadeek Odeh guilty.

THE CLERK: How do you find as to the defendant Mohamed Rashed Daoud Al-'Owhali?

THE FOREPERSON: Mohamed Rashed Daoud Al-'Owhali guilty.

THE CLERK: How do you find as to the defendant Khalfan Khamis Mohamed?

THE FOREPERSON: Khalfan Khamis Mohamed guilty.

THE CLERK: As objective 1, what is your answer?

THE FOREPERSON: Yes. The answer is yes.

THE CLERK: Objective 2?

THE FOREPERSON: Objective 2, the answer is yes.

THE CLERK: Going to Count 3, how do you find as to defendant Odeh?

THE FOREPERSON: Mohamed Sadeek Odeh guilty.

THE CLERK: How do you find as to the defendant Al-'Owhali?

THE CLERK: How do you find as to the defendant Mohamed?

THE FOREPERSON: Defendant Mohamed guilty.

THE CLERK: With respect to objective 1, your answer is?

THE FOREPERSON: Objective 1, the answer is yes.

THE CLERK: With respect to objective 2, your answer is?

THE FOREPERSON: Objective 2, there is no answer.

THE CLERK: On Count 4, how do you find as to defendant El Hage?

THE FOREPERSON: Defendant El Hage guilty.

THE CLERK: How do you find as to defendant Odeh?

THE FOREPERSON: Defendant Odeh guilty.

THE CLERK: How do you find as to defendant Al-'Owhali?

THE FOREPERSON: Defendant Al-'Owhali guilty.

THE CLERK: How do you find as to defendant Mohamed?

THE FOREPERSON: Defendant Mohamed guilty.

THE CLERK: Part A, objective 1. Your answer is?

THE FOREPERSON: The answer is yes.

THE CLERK: Objective 2?

THE FOREPERSON: The answer is yes.

THE CLERK: Part B?

THE FOREPERSON: The answer is yes.

THE CLERK: Part C?

THE FOREPERSON: The answer is yes.

THE CLERK: And part D?

THE FOREPERSON: The answer is yes...

...THE COURT: You found all the defendants guilty on all the counts and have answered the additional questions asked of you as indicated. Mr. Kenneally, would you poll the jury, please.

THE CLERK: Ladies and gentlemen of the jury, you have heard your verdict as it has been recorded.

(Jury polled; each answered in the affirmative)...

... THE COURT: Ladies and gentlemen, you have been very, very patient and your lunch has long been here. My suggestion is that you retire now and have lunch, and then I will have some more words to say to you about tomorrow's proceedings. You may retire. Madame Forelady, would you sign juror No. 1 and date the special verdict form.

THE FOREPERSON: Anywhere in particular?

THE COURT: Last page.

THE FOREPERSON: It is done.

THE COURT: Juror No. 1 and today's date. Thank you. Let us know when you are finished your.

THE JURY: Good afternoon.

THE COURT: First I should say to you there is a long-standing tradition in this court that the judge never expresses to the jury its opinion whether it is in agreement or does not agree with a jury verdict. So please don't assume anything because I make no comment along those lines. But what I do want to say to you on behalf of all of the participants in this case, that we do appreciate how hard you worked and how conscientious you have been, and for that we're all grateful.

Now, if you cast your mind back to January, you will recall that we told you that there were a number of proceedings which may follow your rendition of a verdict; that the proceeding which has just been completed dealt with the question of whether or not guilt had been proven beyond a reasonable doubt.

You have answered that question now, and the next phase relates to punishment. And that phase begins tomorrow, and it begins tomorrow with respect to the defendant Al-'Owhali. And when that is concluded, there will be another phase with respect to the defendant K.K. Mohamed. But you have the afternoon off.

A few reminders. There may be very great pressure by people who know you are on the jury to talk to you, to contact you, to ask you about what went on in the jury room and you reached a particular verdict or not, and please refrain from any such discussions.

Please continue to refrain from reading anything about this case or anything related to this case. There is going to be very heavy media coverage of your verdict and speculation, and please try to avoid reading any of it.

Tomorrow you will be rejoined by your four lost colleagues who were alerted to the fact that they would be called back today. Your verdict is a final verdict and is not open to question, and so I will tell the four alternates, but I now tell you, it is not appropriate for you to revisit with the alternates your verdict, why you reached your verdict or so on.

The inquiry in this next phase is solely with respect to the punishment, beginning tomorrow with Al-'Owhali, whether the appropriate punishment is the imposition of death sentence or the imposition of a sentence of life without possibility of parole. And that is going to be the only issue before you. We will, this afternoon, remove from jury room all of the exhibits. We will leave your notes, the indictment, and the court's charge and the verdict form, but all of the exhibits will be removed from that.

You obviously have to be wondering how long will this next phase take, and I can't give you a definite answer to that. And as soon as we are at a point where I can give youan answer to that which has some meaning, why, we will do that. Certainly shorter than the proceeding — considerably shorter than the proceeding which has just been concluded.

So I thank you again, and we're adjourned until tomorrow morning. You get in at 9:15? 9:30. We adjourned until 9:30 in the morning. Thank you again.

(Jury not present)

THE COURT: The revised draft of the preliminary statements are being handed out now, but I think I have already told you of all of my rulings. And Mr. Fitzgerald, do you have any idea when I will have your brief?

MR. FITZGERALD *(Patrick Fitzgerald, Assistant United States Attorney)*: Yes, I have a very good estimate. I'm about to hand it to your Honor. It's literally the first copy off the printer, so if I could have a copy back. The defense now has it and your Honor has it, and the government does not.

THE COURT: Why don't we adjourn until 3:30, at which time you tell me whether you have anything with respect to the revised preliminary instructions, which, as I have said, I'm going to do orally and not give to the jury, and I will rule on the open matters covered by this brief. So we're adjourned until 3:30.

(Recess)

(In open court)

THE COURT: I distributed a document which is headed "Second Working Draft, May 29, 2001," of the proposed preliminary instructions, marked as Court Exhibit 1 of today's date, and that reflects what I propose to tell the jury tomorrow morning. I leave open for the charging conference, which is now scheduled for Monday at 4:30, whether I should be more explicit with respect to certain matters.

I do say on page 9 in the last paragraph, I first mention briefly before that "you are never required to return a verdict of death." I think that that is an accurate statement, that they are never required to return a verdict of death. I find the law on this area not entirely clear, and some of the decisions, including that of the Eighth Circuit, not entirely persuasive.

We have already told the jury at page 22 of the questionnaire essentially this, over the government's objection, and let me explain why I find the matter not free from doubt. It is unusual in a statute to find Congress talking about preponderance of the evidence and talking about beyond a reasonable doubt and then talking about whether the showing of aggravators significantly outweighs mitigators, and some courts have expressed the view that there has been a conscious decision to make this almost an objective determination.

I keep using the balance sheet analogy, perhaps because I was an accountant before I was a lawyer, and the concern expressed that if a jury can render a verdict which is inconsistent with its weighing of the aggravators and the mitigators, that that creates an opportunity for a subjectivity which some sought to remove from the statute.

If you look at 3593C, it says, "At the sentencing hearing, information may be presented as to any matter relevant to the sentence, including any mitigating or aggravating factor permitted or required to be considered under section 3592," which would suggest that there may be matters relevant to the sentence that are not limited to mitigating or aggravating factors.

And indeed, in my rulings as to what would be admissible at the penalty phase, I have been informed by that language in the statute. And it is for that reason why I include in the preliminary instructions, and will include in the final instructions, although perhaps in different language, the fact that the jury is never required to find death and is not required to find death based on an analysis by the jury which is not necessarily limited to the weighing of the mitigators and the aggravators.

Now, another issue is whether the jury should be told of the consequences of a lack of unanimity with respect to a Gateway factor and an aggravator, and the defendants haverequested that I tell the jury that if they are not in finding a statutory or a Gateway factor, that the consequence is a finding of life. And the government's, if I understand its position, is that I should tell the jury — Well, let me ask the government. Is it the government's position that the jury should be explicitly instructed as to the consequences of a lack of unanimity with respect to statutory or the Gateway factors?

MR. FITZGERALD: The government's position is that we should not instruct the jury on that, that it is a breakdown in the deliberative process if we don't address it until necessary.

MR. RUHNKE *(David Ruhnke, Attorney for Khalfan Khamis Mohamed)*: Your Honor, just to frame the issue properly. We're not just talking about findings of Gateway factors or aggravating factors, we're also talking about the final balancing; that if the jury is not unanimous on the question of whether the aggravating factors substantially or sufficiently outweigh —

THE COURT: I'm not clear of this. What is the government's view if the jury sends a note in which says, "We are not unanimous with respect to whether or not a statutory or Gateway factor has been proven?" what happens then?

MR. FITZGERALD: I think at that point, your Honor, we should fashion an instruction that would tell them to do their best to come to a resolution, but if they cannot, if they have already found that it's a Gateway factor, if you have already found one or more Gateway factors, then proceed on.

THE COURT: Yes.

MR. FITZGERALD: If it's a statutory aggravating factor, if you have already found one or more statutory aggravating factors and you come to the conclusion that you cannot come to a unanimous decision on another one way or the other, then to proceed on.

THE COURT: No, no, no, no. You are assuming that at least one Gateway and one statutory there's unanimity, and you are saying that we don't have to, they don't have to find multiple.

MR. FITZGERALD: Yes.

THE COURT: No. No, I think there is consensus on that. We've just been through a process in the guilt phase where the jury had several options. But suppose there is no single Gateway factor or no single aggravator as to which the jury is unanimous, then what happens?

MR. FITZGERALD: At that point I think we would give the jury and Allen charge, and if they come with no unanimity, then it's over.

THE COURT: What does that mean, "it's over"?

MR. FITZGERALD: My understanding is the jury hangs, and without committing to it, I don't want to be bound to something — it depends which factor it's not decided on. My point —

THE COURT: Let me be explicit as to what my question is. There is at least language, I think it's in Allen, which suggests that if there is a lack of unanimity on any one of the prerequisites to consideration of the death sentence, then the matter is left to the judge; you don't have a hung jury and you don't impanel a new jury. Well, if the matter is left —It's Jones, not Allen.

If the matter is left to the judge, isn't it a fact that the judge can't impose a death sentence?

MR. RUHNKE: No, your honor.

THE COURT: And therefore, isn't the practical consequence of this that before the death sentence can be considered, they must be unanimous? Because if they're not unanimous, then it may be a slightly different process. There may be another step, the reference to the judge, but that the consequence is if they are not unanimous, the death sentence cannot be imposed.

MR. FITZGERALD: I think I follow your Honor. My point is we should not tell the jury that if there is a breakdown in the process, what will happen, because it may invite a breakdown in the process.

THE COURT: I agree with that.

MR. FITZGERALD: Okay.

THE COURT: And that's what I plan to do. I am resisting the suggestion that the jury be told that they must be unanimous, but I am also indicating that if the jury fails to find unanimity as to the Gateway or one statutory, that the practical consequence is the same, and that is the sentence is life.

MR. FITZGERALD: I understand.

MR. COHN *(Frederick H. Cohn, Attorney for Mohamed Rashed Daoud Al-'Owhali)*: May I just, your Honor, say a couple of things? First of all, I thought I heard the government, who is uncharacteristically mumbling, that if they came back with essentially a deadlock notice, you should give an Allen charge.

THE COURT: We don't have to deal with that yet, but —

MR. COHN: It does, because it's responsive sort of to your question, and that is this: That an Allen charge traditionally says you should go back and try again because there's no reason to believe another jury won't come to the same conclusion. Another jury can't come to the same conclusion. It never gets to go to another jury, and therefore, an Allen charge will always be inappropriate. And in my view, a deadlock notice is a verdict.

THE COURT: A deadlock —

MR. COHN: Is a verdict.

THE COURT: A deadlocked jury is a verdict because the consequences of a deadlocked verdict are that the death sentence cannot be imposed.

MR. COHN: That's right. That's my view and that's what a deadlock notice means. Secondly, if your Honor is not going to tell them in your preliminary charge the language about lack of unanimity, I ask that you reconsider your language on page 8 of your preliminary charge just below the typographical error that was corrected. And after you look at it, I'll tell you why.

THE COURT: It's a statute.

MR. COHN: Yes, but it is technically correct, your Honor. But in the context of what you are doing about not telling them that lack of unanimity will result in a verdict of life without parole, it misstates the spirit because it indicates the only way they get life without parole is by unanimity saying no death. And while it does restate the statute and it is technically correct, it's only half the issue and creates a misimpression at this stage, which I think the jury ought not to have. So the answer is it's not incorrect. I just think it's incomplete. And given that you won't give the balancing language later on, you ought to reconsider how you do that. I think that you can fairly tell the jury in place of this that a unanimous verdict for death will result in death and leave it alone.

THE COURT: That's what I say.

MR. COHN: No, you don't. You say a unanimous verdict for life — what you say is if the jury is unanimous — is not justified –

THE COURT: The second part of the language, "must be unanimously and beyond a reasonable doubt before you consider imposition of the death sentence" on page 4.

MR. COHN: But here, your Honor, look on page 8, where it says —

THE COURT: Top of 3, with respect to both the Gateway and the statutory the jury is told that they must be unanimous and beyond a reasonable doubt before they can even consider it.

MR. COHN: Yes, that's right, Judge. But now on page 8 you are on balancing.

THE COURT: Yes.

MR. COHN: And you say, "and if after such balancing the jury unanimously determines that a sentence of death is not justified with regard to it, then he will be sentenced to life imprisonment." And I suggest to you that, your Honor, that while that is correct in terms of the statute, a unanimous verdict, which I'm sure the Court would much prefer, would result in that, it is also true that the failure to reach a unanimous verdict that —

THE COURT: You would like that second sentence to read, "If after such a verdict the jury does not unanimously determine that a sentence of death is justified, the law provides...," that's what you would like?

MR. COHN: I would like that, but I thought your Honor said you won't charge that in this document, and therefore — and if I'm wrong, yes, that's what I would like it to say.

THE COURT: I could strike "unanimously." It will not change the sentence. It could read, "If after such a balance, the jury determines that a sentence of death is not justified."

MR. COHN: No, Judge, I think that doesn't meet it. If it's going to talk about a determination of what is justified, then it should say, "A jury determines that it is justified, then it will result in a verdict of death." That's clear. To charge as to what the jury decides on life without parole is to give an unbalanced charge, because your Honor has said that you will not tell them that failure to be unanimous results in a verdict, and you cannot charge the converse of "death is justified" fairly without including that.

And so what I suggest, if you maintain your position that you will not tell them that lack of unanimity results in a non-death verdict, that you do not say anything about what you say "unanimously finds a jury for death, there will be a verdict of death," but you don't mention the other. That's my view.

THE COURT: You want that sentence stricken?

MR. COHN: I want that sentence stricken, but you may, if you want, put it in unanimity on a death sentence. I don't think you can have that sentence alone without the balancing, with what the actual law is. And if you're not going to charge the actual law —

THE COURT: You are suggesting — I want to be specific. You are suggesting on page 8, the second full paragraph, that the last sentence that begins with "if" be stricken?

MR. COHN: If your Honor is saying you will not charge the language you say you are not charging, the answer is, yes, that's right.

THE COURT: Anybody object to that?

MR. RUHNKE: I don't object to it, your Honor.

THE COURT: We're going to have this over and over again, I'm sure, but I don't know, and that is whether you have a vote on what the jury in the Al-'Owhali phase does or does not hear.

MR. COHN: Your Honor, unfortunately, I think we're in a loop as to Shakespeare's notion about foolish consistencies, because if you are not consistent in the twocharges, we have serious — I think there's an opening for serious mischief.

THE COURT: I think that's true. The law will not change between tomorrow and whenever it is that the K.K. Mohamed proceedings begin.

MR. COHN: And I certainly welcome Mr. Ruhnke's participation in this.

THE COURT: Any objection to my striking that "if" sentence?

MR. FITZGERALD: No, Judge.

THE COURT: I'll strike it. Anything else?

MR. FITZGERALD: Judge, with regard to the language on page 9 that you are including, the second sentence in the last paragraph, you say that the jury is never required to return a verdict of death.

THE COURT: Yes.

MR. FITZGERALD: I have two questions. I know that we haven't resolved it in terms of the final charge. To put it bluntly, will this be held against us in the final charge if it's included in the preliminary charge? To the extent that it was included in the questionnaire, I don't want to sort of go down the slope where when we get to the final charge, it's been in twice and now it's sort of past us.

THE COURT: If you are asking whether it's my intention in the final charge to repeat this thought, the answer is yes. If your question is whether you preserve an objection to my doing so, the answer is also yes.

MR. FITZGERALD: My only thought on that was if your Honor thinks that including it now will make a difference in the final analysis, that we not include it now so that we can preserve the option that your Honor can more or less –

THE COURT: I'm sufficiently firm in my conviction that the jury should be told this.

MR. FITZGERALD: Okay.

MR. RUHNKE: I just have one suggestion at the bottom of page 9.

THE COURT: Yes.

MR. RUHNKE: Actually, that last paragraph that begins "the last thing I wish to explain" is the only time that you tell the jury that they have to be unanimous in order to vote for a sentence of death, and I would ask that you, in the following sentence, beginning, "if the jury does not —"

THE COURT: Yes.

MR. RUHNKE: If the jury does not vote unanimously for a sentence of death, to reiterate that concept.

THE COURT: You think that one sentence is not sufficient?

MR. RUHNKE: Your Honor, it's the only time you tell them that they have to be all in agreement to impose a sentence of death, which is really the crux. The findings are not findings of statutory aggravating factors in this case or non-statutory. But based on my understanding of the facts in this case, they are not going to be much of a hurdle for the jury for some of them. Some of those aggravating factors are subsumed within their guilt verdicts. So I'm asking to emphasize if the jury does not vote unanimously for a sentence of death, it's saying the same thing twice back to back, but repetition is a form of emphasis.

THE COURT: In two sentences.

MR. FITZGERALD: You are asking the bottom of page 9?

MR. RUHNKE: Page 9.

MR. FITZGERALD: Are we talking about just putting the word "unanimous " in that sentence?

THE COURT: Yes.

MR. RUHNKE: If the jury does not vote unanimously for a sentence of death, that's all.

THE COURT: Just repeating what they are told in the preceding sentence. I don't feel strongly on that.

MR. FITZGERALD: Your Honor, I actually think that sentence could be removed, because it goes to the fact that the jury should, we hope, come to a unanimous decision to vote for a death sentence or for life imprisonment. If we took it out, then the paragraph would end, "The last thing I would wish to explain," which would be the last thing, "is that all 12 jurors must agree that death is the appropriate sentence," and they make that point clear.

THE COURT: How about that? I just strike that sentence.

MR. RUHNKE: No, your honor, I don't want that sentence taken out as to what the consequences —

THE COURT: I don't think I have to repeat what is contained in the previous sentence. Anything else with respect to the preliminary instructions? Anything else that –

MR. FITZGERALD: I think your Honor was advised just of a typographical error on page 7 or 8.

THE COURT: Yes, the statutory language was repeated twice.

MR. FITZGERALD: I think on the following page there was some bracketed language which can be removed.

THE COURT: It comes out. Yes. That's fine. I'm just going to anticipate, I try to hedge on the estimate as to how long this will take, but can counsel for Al-'Owhali at this stage give me some —

MR. BAUGH *(David P. Baugh, Attorney for Mohamed Rashed Daoud Al-'Owhali)*: About two days, your Honor.

THE COURT: Two days?

MR. BAUGH: Two days. About two days for the defense mitigation case, yes.

THE COURT: We're not sitting Friday, so we will have Wednesday, Thursday — this should go to the jury towards the end of next week.

MR. BAUGH: Yes.

MR. FITZGERALD: Yes, your Honor. I would say it this way. If we thought that the victim impact witnesses should come out to be about two days, there's a little bit a few other witnesses, but not a lot. If we're starting that after the openings tomorrow, we're hoping that since we're sitting Wednesday, Thursday, that the government should rest probably Monday, probably Monday afternoon. With Mr. Baugh going two days, that might take us to Wednesday, and since we'll have a rebuttal case, it appears, on prison conditions, the proof may end next Thursday. So it could possibly be that the argument spills over to the following week.

THE COURT: All right. That's fine. It's helpful to know that. We have had some recurring discovery issues, including the military, and I have not — the shoe has not dropped so far as I am concerned, but —

MR. BAUGH: The military has given us all that the military said they can give us and that's that, and we're just going to have to — that's it.

THE COURT: Very well. I can't compel any party to litigation to produce that which it cannot produce.

MR. BAUGH: I didn't go that far, Judge. But, yes, I understand it.

THE COURT: There is no ruling from the court that you now seek with respect to that issue?

MR. BAUGH: That is correct, your Honor.

THE COURT: All right. Mr. Ruhnke?

MR. RUHNKE: Your Honor, there is one issue that we've been trying to determine through Mr. Garcia and the government what happened to the videotape on November 1, 2000 that should have been played and recorded on 10 South. We're going to need a resolution of that soon or hearing or something to determine, because we are getting conflicting verses. It is not Mr. Garcia's fault. He's given the same sources we're getting. People tell us different things.

MR. GARCIA: Mr. Ruhnke is correct. He sent me a letter. The government hasn't had an opportunity to respond to it. We will respond to it as soon as we can, and after that we may perhaps need something from the court or we may not.

MR. RUHNKE: Okay.

MR. FITZGERALD: And on the lines of discovery, we had a discussion with counsel for Khalfan Mohamed. I understand that there may be four, five or six expert witnesses for which we have not yet received discovery, but I understand we will receive it tomorrow.

MR. RUHNKE: Yes, by close of business tomorrow.

THE COURT: All right. Anything else? We're adjourned then until — Mr. Cohn.

MR. COHN: One sheer housekeeping issue that I want to alert the Court to, and that is that Mr. Ruhnke has asked, because he's so impressed by her acumen, that he use my paralegal during his penalty phase and I'm just — I said yes, and just so when you see the bills from me, she's on my payroll, but she'll be working actually for him and you won't see bills from him for her time. That's all. I'm just not going to shift her payroll to his to do that and that's all I'm suggesting.

THE COURT: I have no problem with that. Government have any problem?

MR. FITZGERALD: No.

THE COURT: You are going to be seated at the first seats?

MR. COHN: We are going to move over, yes.

THE COURT: And the rest of the table is going to be blank, right?

MR. RUHNKE: Do not intend to be at counsel table during the proceedings. We do not expect Mr. Khalfan Mohamed to be in court. We certainly may witness the parties proceedings and all parts of it, but we will not be at counsel table.

THE COURT: Anything else?

MR. FITZGERALD: Your Honor, may I inquire as to any of the issues not yet finally resolved such as what could be argued about. Does counsel for Al-'Owhali intend to argue jury nullification in opening?

MR. BAUGH: No.

MR. FITZGERALD: Fine.

MR. BAUGH: Nullification in this case?

MR. FITZGERALD: Nullification.

THE COURT: At least one court, in talking about some of the issues we have discussed has invoked the concept of jury nullification, has said that to permit a jury to find against the death penalty despite the weighing of the aggravators and mitigators would be to sanction the jury nullification. I don't agree with that.

MR. COHN: I don't either, Judge. And in the traditional terms of nullification, this is not the case.

THE COURT: Yes. I agree. All right. I take it that there is nothing further counsel needs prior to opening statements tomorrow. We're adjourned then until 9:30 tomorrow morning.

MR. FITZGERALD: Yes, Judge. Thank you.

DOCUMENT No. II

CONVENTION FOR THE SUPPRESSION OF UNLAWFUL ACTS AGAINST THE SAFETY OF CIVIL AVIATION

SIGNED AT MONTREAL ON 23 SEPTEMBER 1971
ENTRY INTO FORCE: 26 January 1973

THE STATES PARTIES to the Convention

Considering that unlawful acts against the safety of civil aviation jeopardize the safety of persons and property, seriously affect the operation of air services, and undermine the confidence of the peoples of the world in the safety of civil aviation;

Considering that the occurrence of such acts is a matter of grave concern;

Considering that, for the purpose of deterring such acts, there is an urgent need to provide appropriate measures for punishment of offenders;

Have agreed as follows:

Article 1

    1.   Any person commits an offence if he unlawfully and intentionally:
        a.   performs an act of violence against a person on board an aircraft in flight if that act is likely to endanger the safety of that aircraft; or
        b.   destroys an aircraft in service or causes damage to such an aircraft which renders it incapable of flight or which is likely to endanger its safety in flight; or
        c.   places or causes to be placed on an aircraft in service, by any means whatsoever, a device or substance which is likely to destroy that aircraft, or to cause damage to it which renders it incapable of flight, or to cause damage to it which is likely to endanger its safety in flight; or
        d.   destroys or damages air navigation facilities or interferes with their operation, if any such act is likely to endanger the safety of aircraft in flight; or
        e.   communicates information which he knows to be false, thereby endangering the safety of an aircraft in flight.
    2.   Any person also commits an offence if he:
        a.   attempts to commit any of the offences mentioned in paragraph 1 of this Article; or

   b. is an accomplice of a person who commits or attempts to commit any such offence.

Article 2
For the purposes of this Convention:
   a. an aircraft is considered to be in flight at any time from the moment when all its external doors are closed following embarkation until the moment when any such door is opened for disembarkation; in the case of a forced landing, the flight shall be deemed to continue until the competent authorities take over the responsibility for the aircraft and for persons and property on board;
   b. an aircraft is considered to be in service from the beginning of the pre-flight preparation of the aircraft by ground personnel or by the crew for a specific flight until twenty-four hours after any landing; the period of service shall, in any event, extend for the entire period during which the aircraft is in flight as defined in paragraph (a) of this Article.

Article 3
Each Contracting State undertakes to make the offences mentioned in Article 1 punishable by severe penalties.

Article 4
   1. This Convention shall not apply to aircraft used in military, customs or police services.
   2. In the cases contemplated in subparagraphs (a), (b), (c) and (e) of paragraph 1 of Article 1, this Convention shall apply, irrespective of whether the aircraft is engaged in an international or domestic flight, only if:
       a. the place of take-off or landing, actual or intended, of the aircraft is situated outside the territory of the State of registration of that aircraft; or
       b. the offence is committed in the territory of a State other than the State of registration of the aircraft.
   3. Notwithstanding paragraph 2 of this Article, in the cases contemplated in subparagraphs (a), (b), (c) and (e) of paragraph 1 of Article 1, this Convention shall also apply if the offender or the alleged offender is found in the territory of a State other than the State of registration of the aircraft.
   4. With respect to the States mentioned in Article 9 and in the cases mentioned in subparagraphs (a), (b), (c) and (e) of paragraph 1 of Article 1, this Convention shall not apply if the places referred to in subparagraph (a) of paragraph 2 of this Article are situated within the territory of the same State where that State is one of those referred to in Article 9, unless the offence is committed or the offender or alleged offender is found in the territory of a State other than that State.
   5. In the cases contemplated in subparagraph (d) of paragraph 1 of Article 1, this Convention shall apply only if the air navigation facilities are used in

international air navigation.

6. The provisions of paragraphs 2, 3, 4 and 5 of this Article shall also apply in the cases contemplated in paragraph 2 of Article 1.

Article 5

1. Each Contracting State shall take such measures as may be necessary to establish its jurisdiction over the offences in the following cases:
    a. when the offence is committed in the territory of that State;
    b. when the offence is committed against or on board an aircraft registered in that State;
    c. when the aircraft on board which the offence is committed lands in its territory with the alleged offender still on board;
    d. when the offence is committed against or on board an aircraft leased without crew to a lessee who has his principal place of business or, if the lessee has no such place of business, his permanent residence, in that State.
2. Each Contracting State shall likewise take such measures as may be necessary to establish its jurisdiction over the offences mentioned in Article 1, paragraph 1 (a), (b) and (c), and in Article 1, paragraph 2, in so far as that paragraph relates to those offences, in the case where the alleged offender is present in its territory and it does not extradite him pursuant to Article 8 to any of the States mentioned in paragraph 1 of this Article.
3. This Convention does not exclude any criminal jurisdiction exercised in accordance with national law.

Article 6

1. Upon being satisfied that the circumstances so warrant, any Contracting State in the territory of which the offender or the alleged offender is present, shall take him into custody or take other measures to ensure his presence. The custody and other measures shall be as provided in the law of that State but may only be continued for such time as is necessary to enable any criminal or extradition proceedings to be instituted.
2. Such State shall immediately make a preliminary enquiry into the facts.
3. Any person in custody pursuant to paragraph 1 of this Article shall be assisted in communicating immediately with the nearest appropriate representative of the State of which he is a national.
4. When a State, pursuant to this Article, has taken a person into custody, it shall immediately notify the States mentioned in Article 5, paragraph 1, the State of nationality of the detained person and, if it considers it advisable, any other interested State of the fact that such person is in custody and of the circumstances which warrant his detention. The State which makes the preliminary enquiry contemplated in paragraph 2 of this Article shall promptly report its findings to the said States and shall indicate whether it intends to exercise jurisdiction.

Article 7

The Contracting State in the territory of which the alleged offender is found shall, if it does not extradite him, be obliged, without exception whatsoever and whether or not the offence was committed in its territory, to submit the case to its competent authorities for the purpose of prosecution. Those authorities shall take their decision in the same manner as in the case of any ordinary offence of a serious nature under the law of that State.

Article 8

1. The offences shall be deemed to be included as extraditable offences in any extradition treaty existing between Contracting States. Contracting States undertake to include the offences as extraditable offences in every extradition treaty to be concluded between them.
2. If a Contracting State which makes extradition conditional on the existence of a treaty receives a request for extradition from another Contracting State with which it has no extradition treaty, it may at its option consider this Convention as the legal basis for extradition in respect of the offences. Extradition shall be subject to the other conditions provided by the law of the requested State.
3. Contracting States which do not make extradition conditional on the existence of a treaty shall recognize the offences as extraditable offences between themselves subject to the conditions provided by the law of the requested State.
4. Each of the offences shall be treated, for the purpose of extradition between Contracting States, as if it had been committed not only in the place in which it occurred but also in the territories of the States required to establish their jurisdiction in accordance with Article 5, paragraph 1 (b), (c) and (d).

Article 9

The Contracting States which establish joint air transport operating organizations or international operating agencies, which operate aircraft which are subject to joint or international registration shall, by appropriate means, designate for each aircraft the State among them which shall exercise the jurisdiction and have the attributes of the State of registration for the purpose of this Convention and shall give notice thereof to the International Civil Aviation Organization which shall communicate the notice to all States Parties to this Convention.

Article 10

1. Contracting States shall, in accordance with international and national law, endeavour to take all practicable measure for the purpose of preventing the offences mentioned in Article 1.
2. When, due to the commission of one of the offences mentioned in Article 1, a flight has been delayed or interrupted, any Contracting State in whose territory the aircraft or passengers or crew are present shall facilitate the

continuation of the journey of the passengers and crew as soon as practicable, and shall without delay return the aircraft and its cargo to the persons lawfully entitled to possession.

Article 11

1. Contracting States shall afford one another the greatest measure of assistance in connection with criminal proceedings brought in respect of the offences. The law of the State requested shall apply in all cases.
2. The provisions of paragraph 1 of this Article shall not affect obligations under any other treaty, bilateral or multilateral, which governs or will govern, in whole or in part, mutual assistance in criminal matters.

Article 12

Any Contracting State having reason to believe that one of the offences mentioned in Article 1 will be committed shall, in accordance with its national law, furnish any relevant information in its possession to those States which it believes would be the States mentioned in Article 5, paragraph 1.

Article 13

Each Contracting State shall in accordance with its national law report to the Council of the International Civil Aviation Organization as promptly as possible any relevant information in its possession concerning: (a) the circumstances of the offence;(b) the action taken pursuant to Article 10, paragraph 2; (c) the measures taken in relation to the offender or the alleged offender and, in particular, the results of any extradition proceedings or other legal proceedings.

Article 14

1. Any dispute between two or more Contracting States concerning the interpretation or application of this Convention which cannot be settled through negotiation, shall, at the request of one of them, be submitted to arbitration. If within six months from the date of the request for arbitration the Parties are unable to agree on the organization of the arbitration, any one of those Parties may refer the dispute to the International Court of Justice by request in conformity with the Statute of the Court.
2. Each State may at the time of signature or ratification of this Convention or accession thereto, declare that it does not consider itself bound by the preceding paragraph. The other Contracting States shall not be bound by the preceding paragraph with respect to any Contracting State having made such a reservation.
3. Any Contracting State having made a reservation in accordance with the preceding paragraph may at any time withdraw this reservation by notification to the Depositary Governments.

Article 15

1. This Convention shall be open for signature at Montreal on 23 September 1971, by States participating in the International Conference on Air Law

held at Montreal from 8 to 23 September 1971 (hereinafter referred to as the Montreal Conference). After 10 October 1971, the Convention shall be open to all States for signature in Moscow, London and Washington. Any State which does not sign this Convention before its entry into force in accordance with paragraph 3 of this Article may accede to it at any time.

2. This Convention shall be subject to ratification by the signatory States. Instruments of ratification and instruments of accession shall be deposited with the Governments of the Union of Soviet Socialist Republics, the United Kingdom of Great Britain and Northern Ireland, and the United States of America, which are hereby designated the Depositary Governments.

3. This Convention shall enter into force thirty days following the date of the deposit of instruments of ratification by ten States signatory to this Convention which participated in the Montreal Conference.

4. For other States, this Convention shall enter into force on the date of entry into force of this Convention in accordance with paragraph 3 of this Article, or thirty days following the date of deposit of their instruments of ratification or accession, whichever is later.

5. The Depositary Governments shall promptly inform all signatory and acceding States of the date of each signature, the date of deposit of each instrument of ratification or accession, the date of entry into force of this Convention, and other notices.

6. As soon as this Convention comes into force, it shall be registered by the Depositary Governments pursuant to Article 102 of the Convention on International Civil Aviation (Chicago, 1944).

Article 16

1. Any Contracting State may denounce this Convention by written notification to the Depositary Governments.

2. Denunciation shall take effect six months following the date on which notification is received by the Depositary Governments.

IN WITNESS WHEREOF the undersigned Plenipotentiaries, being duly authorized thereto by their Governments, have signed this Convention.

DONE at Montreal, this twenty-third day of September, one thousand nine hundred and seventy-one, in three originals, each being drawn up in four authentic texts in the English, French, Russian and Spanish languages.

DOCUMENT No. 12

Ottawa Ministerial Declaration on Countering Terrorism

Released at the Ottawa Ministerial on December 12, 1995.

Preamble

1. We met in Ottawa on December 12, as agreed upon at the Halifax Summit in June 1995 by the Heads of State and Government of the seven most industrialized nations and Russia, to discuss specific, cooperative measures to deter, prevent and investigate terrorist acts. We fulfilled our mandate and are united in our determination to work together with the entire international community to combat terrorism in all its forms.

G-7/P-8 History

2. Since 1978, the G-7 partners have worked together to counter terrorism. Their cooperation has been instrumental in obtaining agreements in many fora on issues such as transportation security and the exchange of information. There has also been extensive work by the G-7, over the course of the last two decades on ensuring that loopholes in national legislation are closed, and that countries act in concert in denying arms and free movement to terrorists. These efforts have shown leadership to the international community as a whole. Russia's experience and participation is of great assistance in supporting the efforts of Summit partners in combating terrorism.

Review of Recent Trends

3. We began by exchanging views on recent major terrorist events including the Tokyo subway attacks, the bombing in Oklahoma City, the hostage taking in Budennovsk, major terrorist attacks against the Middle East peace process (including the assassination of Yitzhak Rabin), the persistent attacks by the ETA, the bombing campaign in France, and the bombings in Riyadh and Islamabad. These and other events point to a number of trends including an upsurge in domestic terrorism, an increase in hostage taking and indiscriminate violence by religious extremists and apocalyptic groups which practice terrorism, as well as continuing examples of attacks on tourists and the export regional conflicts. These developments have been accompanied by a continuing use of conventional weapons, in particular those designed for massive explosions, and by a new and worrying use of non-conventional, for example chemical, weapons. We call for political groups to use dialogue, exercise tolerance and repudiate the use of terrorism. We offer dialogue to those who reject violence and respect the law. Those who attempt to achieve their aims through violence will, however, meet with our strongest resolve and be held accountable for their criminal acts.

Improved International Cooperation

4. We are determined to work together in the international community, with international organizations, institutions and other fora to fight terrorism. We will work in all organizations of the UN family, the General Assembly and all other

appropriate fora to identify and adopt practical measures to fight terrorism, including where necessary legal instruments. We will work bilaterally and multilaterally, taking full advantage of such organizations as Interpol, to improve measures against terrorism. We will propose and support information sharing with and among members of other regional organizations. We welcome, for example, the efforts made in the context of the recent sub-regional meeting in Buenos Aires, and the prospects for the OAS Ministerial meetings on terrorism.

International and Domestic Legal Framework

5. We call on all states to strive to become party to the existing international conventions concerned with countering terrorism and urgently bring their domestic legislation into harmony with those conventions by the year 2000. It is our view that strong laws, effectively enforced, continue to be a convincing deterrent in combating terrorism. We call upon all States that assist terrorists to renounce terrorism and to deny financial support. All perpetrators of terrorist acts must be brought to swift justice. Stronger law enforcement cooperation and mutual legal assistant are among the measures best suited to deter and prevent international terrorist acts and punish terrorists. We have decided to have our experts continue to explore new ways of enhancing the current international legal regime, in particular to address new forms of terrorism. To avoid terrorists escaping punishment we call on all States to strengthen their domestic, bilateral or international extradition arrangements and to consider adoption of additional instruments.

Exchange of Expertise and Information to Prevent Terrorist Acts

6. One of the more effective tools we have to counter terrorism is sharing information among ourselves and with others. Terrorists operate secretively. Intelligence concerning terrorists, their movements, their support and their weapons are essential for countering their activities and enforcing laws against terrorism. Increasing the sharing of expertise, information, and intelligence between our countries and among the international community, is essential for countering terrorism. With an aim to preventing terrorist acts we propose to:

- share our technical knowledge, intelligence, forecasts of threats and activities and information on different tactics and methods, means, of terrorists through closer bilateral and other forms of co-operation among police and security agencies and other relevant authorities;
- share more widely information, including consular travel advisories, on countries where there is a threat to our citizens abroad;
- share expertise on the protection of public buildings and facilities;
- share information on fanatical and apocalyptic terrorist groups;
- increase counter-terrorism training and assistance;
- improve procedures for the tracing and tracking of suspected terrorists; and
- enhance information sharing on major terrorist incidents in a timely fashion.

Taking of Hostages

7. We noted the sinister increase in the taking of hostages by terrorists and other criminals. We call on all states that have not already done so to adhere to the 1979

International Convention Against the Taking of Hostages. We call on all States to condemn the practice of hostage-taking; to refuse to make substantive concessions to hostage-takers; to work for the safety of those taken hostage; to deny to hostage takers any benefits from their criminal acts; to work tirelessly together to resolve ongoing hostage cases, and to bring to justice those responsible.

New Threats Related to Weapons of Mass Destruction

8. We intend to strengthen measures to prevent the use of weapons designed to induce high casualty rates and encourage others to do likewise. We also noted with deep concern the chemical gas attacks on the Tokyo subway system which caused deaths and widespread injury. We urge all Governments to take the strongest measures to prevent toxic chemicals and biological agents from getting into the hands of terrorists and to adopt appropriate national legislation and controls in line with the Chemical Weapons and Biological and Toxin Weapons Conventions. We invite countries who have already taken such measures to share their expertise with those who wish to take such measures. We have agreed to exchange information among ourselves and with others. We will implement measures to deter and respond to chemical and biological terrorist threats and incidents and to investigate and prevent the illicit production, trafficking, possession and use of such sub-stances. We encourage other governments to join in this effort. We ask our experts in this area to meet and further pursue development of these measures. We have asked the experts concerned with the preparation of the Moscow Summit on Nuclear Safety and Security to be held in spring of 1996 to also consider measures, taking into account the 1980 Convention on the Physical Protection of Nuclear MateriAl, to prevent nuclear materiAl falling into the hands of terrorists.

Preventing the Movement of Terrorists

9. Effective entry controls, assisted by new and emerging technologies, will help prevent the spread of terrorism. We, therefore, propose to cooperate further in the development of travel documents which are more difficult to falsify and to increase joint training and information sharing among ourselves, and with others, on fraudulent travel document detection and immigration control. In this regard we recognized the importance of the ICAO standards being adopted and urge all countries to implement them. We also call on all States to enforce sanctions against the use of false and fraudulent documents. Within the framework of international law and in our own jurisdictions we will deny entry to all those, including diplo-mats, who, on the basis of available information, are involved in terrorist activities and thereby pose a threat to national security.

Transportation Security

10. We have agreed to work together and with others to continue to improve security of all forms of transportation around the world. To date there are seven international conventions and treaties related to transportation security which have had a marked impact on maritime and aviation security. We encourage the current work of the International Civil Aviation Organization (ICAO) and the Interna-tional Maritime Organization (IMO) to develop common standards for security procedures to boost security in the aviation and maritime fields. Their resolutions must be implemented by the entire international community with an aim of fighting international mechanisms in the fight against terrorism.

Public Facilities

11. Terrorists take advantage of the openness and vulnerability of public facilities, particularly in free societies. As anti-terrorist measures have become more successful, terrorists are looking to new targets of opportunity in their attacks. In order to reduce the risks to our citizens, we pledge to cooperate further and to share information and experiences concerning the protection and securing of possible targets such as transport systems, information systems, public utilities, and public buildings including diplomatic premises.

Terrorism Funding

12. We have agreed to pursue measures aimed at depriving terrorists of their sources of finance. We encourage all States to take action in cooperation with other States, to prevent terrorists from raising funds that in any way support terrorist activities and explore the means of tracking and freezing assets used by terrorist groups.

Conclusion and Guidelines for Action

13. We are determined as a group to continue to provide leadership on this issue to the international community, using bilateral and multilateral measures and agreements to counter terrorism. We will continue to develop specific, cooperative measures to deter, prevent, and investigate terrorist acts and to bring terrorist to justice. We will take action to implement the guidelines set forth in this declaration and summarized as follows:

- calling on all states to strive to join existing international treaties on terrorism by the year 2000;
- promoting mutual legal assistance and extradition;
- strengthening the sharing of intelligence and information on terrorism;
- pursuing measures to prevent terrorist use of nuclear, chemical and biological materials;
- urging all States to refuse to make substantive concessions to hostage takers and to ensure those responsible are brought to justice;
- inhibiting the movement of terrorists and enhancing measures to prevent the falsification of documents;
- strengthening protection of aviation, maritime and other transportation systems against terrorism;
- countering terrorist attacks against public facilities and infrastructures; depriving terrorists of funds; and
- increasing counter-terrorism training and assistance.

DOCUMENT No. 13

UN RESOLUTION 52/164
International Convention for the Suppression of Terrorist Bombings

UNITED NATIONS GENERAL ASSEMBLY
A/RES/52/164
09 January 1998
Fifty-second session
Agenda item 152

RESOLUTION ADOPTED BY THE GENERAL ASSEMBLY
[on the report of the Sixth Committee (A/52/653)]
International Convention for the Suppression of Terrorist Bombings

The General Assembly,
Recalling its resolution 49/60 of 9 December 1994, by which it adopted the
Declaration on Measures to Eliminate International Terrorism, and its resolution
51/210 of 17 December 1996,
Having considered the text of the draft convention for the suppression of terrorist
bombings prepared by the Ad Hoc Committee established by General Assembly
resolution 51/210 of 17 December 1996[1] and the Working Group of the Sixth
Committee,[2]
1. Adopts the International Convention for the Suppression of Terrorist Bombings
annexed to the present resolution, and decides to open it for signature at United
Nations Headquarters in New York from 12 January 1998 until 31 December
1999;
2. Urges all States to sign and ratify, accept or approve or accede to the Convention.
72nd plenary meeting
15 December 1997
ANNEX
International Convention for the Suppression of Terrorist Bombings

The States Parties to this Convention,
Having in mind the purposes and principles of the Charter of the United Nations
concerning the maintenance of international peace and security and the promotion
of good-neighbourliness and friendly relations and cooperation among States,
Deeply concerned about the worldwide escalation of acts of terrorism in all its
forms and manifestations,

---

[1] *See Official Records of the General Assembly, Fifty-second Session,Supplement No. 37 (A/52/37).*
[2] *See A/C.6/52/L.3, annex I.*

Recalling the Declaration on the Occasion of the Fiftieth Anniversary of the
United Nations of 24 October 1995, [2]
Recalling also the Declaration on Measures to Eliminate International Terrorism,
annexed to General Assembly resolution 49/60 of 9 December 1994, in which,
inter alia, "the States Members of the United Nations solemnly reaffirm their
unequivocal condemnation of all acts, methods and practices of terrorism as
criminal and unjustifiable, wherever and by whomever committed, including those
which jeopardize the friendly relations among States and peoples and threaten the
territorial integrity and security of States",
Noting that the Declaration also encouraged States "to review urgently the scope of
the existing international legal provisions on the prevention, repression and
elimination of terrorism in all its forms and manifestations, with the aim of
ensuring that there is a comprehensive legal framework covering all aspects of the
matter",
Recalling General Assembly resolution 51/210 of 17 December 1996 and the
Declaration to Supplement the 1994 Declaration on Measures to Eliminate International Terrorism annexed thereto,
Noting that terrorist attacks by means of explosives or other lethal devices have
become increasingly widespread,
Noting also that existing multilateral legal provisions do not adequately address
these attacks,
Being convinced of the urgent need to enhance international cooperation between
States in devising and adopting effective and practical measures for the prevention
of such acts of terrorism and for the prosecution and punishment of their perpetrators,
Considering that the occurrence of such acts is a matter of grave concern to the
international community as a whole,
Noting that the activities of military forces of States are governed by rules of
international law outside the framework of this Convention and that the exclusion
of certain actions from the coverage of this Convention does not condone or make
lawful otherwise unlawful acts, or preclude prosecution under other laws,
Have agreed as follows:

Article 1

For the purposes of this Convention:
1. "State or government facility" includes any permanent or temporary facility or
conveyance that is used or occupied by representatives of a State, members of
Government, the legislature or the judiciary or by officials or employees of a State
or any other public authority or entity or by employees or officials of an intergovernmental organization in connection with their official duties.
2. "Infrastructure facility" means any publicly or privately owned facility providing
or distributing services for the benefit of the public, such as water, sewage, energy,
fuel or communications.
3. "Explosive or other lethal device" means:
   (a) An explosive or incendiary weapon or device that is designed, or has the

[2] *See resolution 50/6.*

capability, to cause death, serious bodily injury or substantial material damage; or

(b) A weapon or device that is designed, or has the capability, to cause death, serious bodily injury or substantial material damage through the release, dissemination or impact of toxic chemicals, biological agents or toxins or similar substances or radiation or radioactive material.

4. "Military forces of a State" means the armed forces of a State which are organized, trained and equipped under its internal law for the primary purpose of national defence or security and persons acting in support of those armed forces who are under their formal command, control and responsibility.

5. "Place of public use" means those parts of any building, land, street, waterway or other location that are accessible or open to members of the public, whether continuously, periodically or occasionally, and encompasses any commercial, business, cultural, historical, educational, religious, governmental, entertainment, recreational or similar place that is so accessible or open to the public.

6. "Public transportation system" means all facilities, conveyances and instrumentalities, whether publicly or privately owned, that are used in or for publicly available services for the transportation of persons or cargo.

Article 2

1. Any person commits an offence within the meaning of this Convention if that person unlawfully and intentionally delivers, places, discharges or detonates an explosive or other lethal device in, into or against a place of public use, a State or government facility, a public transportation system or an infrastructure facility:

(a) With the intent to cause death or serious bodily injury; or

(b) With the intent to cause extensive destruction of such a place, facility or system, where such destruction results in or is likely to result in major economic loss.

2. Any person also commits an offence if that person attempts to commit an offence as set forth in paragraph 1 of the present article.

3. Any person also commits an offence if that person:

(a) Participates as an accomplice in an offence as set forth in paragraph 1 or 2 of the present article; or

(b) Organizes or directs others to commit an offence as set forth in paragraph 1 or 2 of the present article; or

(c) In any other way contributes to the commission of one or more offences as set forth in paragraph 1 or 2 of the present article by a group of persons acting with a common purpose; such contribution shall be intentional and either be made with the aim of furthering the general criminal activity or purpose of the group or be made in the knowledge of the intention of the group to commit the offence or offences concerned.

Article 3

This Convention shall not apply where the offence is committed within a single State, the alleged offender and the victims are nationals of that State, the alleged offender is found in the territory of that State and no other State has a basis under article 6, paragraph 1 or paragraph 2, of this Convention to exercise jurisdiction, except that the provisions of articles 10 to 15 shall, as appropriate, apply in those cases.

Article 4

Each State Party shall adopt such measures as may be necessary:
  (a) To establish as criminal offences under its domestic law the offences set forth in article 2 of this Convention;
  (b) To make those offences punishable by appropriate penalties which take into account the grave nature of those offences.

Article 5

Each State Party shall adopt such measures as may be necessary, including, where appropriate, domestic legislation, to ensure that criminal acts within the scope of this Convention, in particular where they are intended or calculated to provoke a state of terror in the general public or in a group of persons or particular persons, are under no circumstances justifiable by considerations of a political, philosophical, ideological, racial, ethnic, religious or other similar nature and are punished by penalties consistent with their grave nature.

Article 6

1. Each State Party shall take such measures as may be necessary to establish its jurisdiction over the offences set forth in article 2 when:
  (a) The offence is committed in the territory of that State; or
  (b) The offence is committed on board a vessel flying the flag of that State or an aircraft which is registered under the laws of that State at the time the offence is committed; or
  (c) The offence is committed by a national of that State.
2. A State Party may also establish its jurisdiction over any of that when:
  (a) The offence is committed against a national of that State; or
  (b) The offence is committed against a State or government facility of that State abroad, including an embassy or other diplomatic or consular premises of that State; or
  (c) The offence is committed by a stateless person who has his or her habitual residence in the territory of that State; or
  (d) The offence is committed in an attempt to compel that State to do or abstain from doing any act; or (e) The offence is committed on board an aircraft which is operated by the Government of that State.
3. Upon ratifying, accepting, approving or acceding to this Convention,each State Party shall notify the Secretary-General of the United Nations of the jurisdiction it has established under its domestic law in accordance with paragraph 2 of the present article. Should any change take place, the State Party concerned shall immediately notify the Secretary-General.
4. Each State Party shall likewise take such measures as may be necessary to establish its jurisdiction over the offences set forth in article 2 in cases where the alleged offender is present in its territory and it does not extradite that person to any of the States Parties which have established their jurisdiction in accordance with paragraph 1 or 2 of the present article.
5. This Convention does not exclude the exercise of any criminal jurisdiction established by a State Party in accordance with its domestic law.

Article 7

1. Upon receiving information that a person who has committed or who is alleged to have committed an offence as set forth in article 2 may be present in its territory, the State Party concerned shall take such measures as may be necessary under its domestic law to investigate the facts contained in the information.

2. Upon being satisfied that the circumstances so warrant, the State Party in whose territory the offender or alleged offender is present shall take the appropriate measures under its domestic law so as to ensure that person's presence for the purpose of prosecution or extradition.

3. Any person regarding whom the measures referred to in paragraph 2 of the present article are being taken shall be entitled to:

    (a) Communicate without delay with the nearest appropriate representative of the State of which that person is a national or which is otherwise entitled to protect that person's rights or, if that person is a stateless person, the State in the territory of which that person habitually resides;

    (b) Be visited by a representative of that State;

    (c) Be informed of that person's rights under subparagraphs (a) and(b).

4. The rights referred to in paragraph 3 of the present article shall be exercised in conformity with the laws and regulations of the State in he territory of which the offender or alleged offender is present, subject to the provision that the said laws and regulations must enable full effect to be given to the purposes for which the rights accorded under paragraph 3 are intended.

5. The provisions of paragraphs 3 and 4 of the present article shall be without prejudice to the right of any State Party having a claim to jurisdiction in accordance with article 6, subparagraph 1 (c) or 2 (c),to invite the International Committee of the Red Cross to communicate with and visit the alleged offender.

6. When a State Party, pursuant to the present article, has taken a person into custody, it shall immediately notify, directly or through the Secretary-General of the United Nations, the States Parties which have established jurisdiction in accordance with article 6, paragraphs 1 and 2, and, if it considers it advisable, any other interested States Parties, of the fact that that person is in custody and of he circumstances which warrant that person's detention. The State which makes the investigation contemplated in paragraph 1 of the present article shall promptly inform the said States Parties of its findings andshall indicate whether it intends to exercise jurisdiction.

Article 8

1. The State Party in the territory of which the alleged offender the is present shall, in cases to which article 6 applies, if it does not extradite that person, be obliged, without exception whatsoever and whether or not the offence was committed in its territory, to submit the case without undue delay to its competent authorities for the purpose of prosecution, through proceedings in accordance with the laws of the. Those authorities shall take their decision in the same manner as in the case of any other offence of a grave nature under the law of that State.

2. Whenever a State Party is permitted under its domestic law to extradite or otherwise surrender one of its nationals only upon the condition that the person will be returned to that State to serve the sentence imposed as a result of the trial

or proceeding for which the extradition or surrender of the person was sought, and this State and the State seeking the extradition of the person agree with this option and other terms they may deem appropriate, such a conditional extradition or surrender shall be sufficient to discharge the obligation set forth in paragraph 1 of the present article.

Article 9

1. The offences set forth in article 2 shall be deemed to be included as extraditable offences in any extradition treaty existing between any of the States Parties before the entry into force of this Convention. States Parties undertake to include such offences as extraditable offences in every extradition treaty to be subsequently concluded between them.

2. When a State Party which makes extradition conditional on the existence of a treaty receives a request for extradition from another State Party with which it has no extradition treaty, the requested State Party may, at its option, consider this Convention as a legal basis for extradition in respect of the offences set forth in article 2. Extradition shall be subject to the other conditions provided by the law of the requested State.

3. States Parties which do not make extradition conditional on the existence of a treaty shall recognize the offences set forth in article 2 as extraditable offences between themselves, subject to the conditions provided by the law of the requested State.

4. If necessary, the offences set forth in article 2 shall be treated, for the purposes of extradition between States Parties, as if they had been committed not only in the place in which they occurred but also in the territory of the States that have established jurisdiction in accordance with article 6, paragraphs 1 and 2.5. The provisions of all extradition treaties and arrangements between States Parties with regard to offences set forth in article 2 shall be deemed to be modified as between State Parties to the extent that they are incompatible with this Convention.

Article 10

1. States Parties shall afford one another the greatest measure of assistance in connection with investigations or criminal or extradition proceedings brought in respect of the offences set forth in article 2, including assistance in obtaining evidence at their disposal necessary for the proceedings.

2. States Parties shall carry out their obligations under paragraph 1 of the present article in conformity with any treaties or other arrangements on mutual legal assistance that may exist between them. In the absence of such treaties or arrangements, States Parties shall afford one another assistance in accordance with their domestic law.

Article 11

None of the offences set forth in article 2 shall be regarded, for the purposes of extradition or mutual legal assistance, as a political offence or as an offence connected with a political offence or as an offence inspired by political motives. Accordingly, a request for extradition or for mutual legal assistance based on such an offence may not be refused on the sole ground that it concerns a political offence or an offence connected with a political offence or an offence inspired by political motives.

Article 12

Nothing in this Convention shall be interpreted as imposing an obligation to extradite or to afford mutual legal assistance, if the requested State Party has substantial grounds for believing that the request for extradition for offences set forth in article 2 or for mutual legal assistance with respect to such offences has been made for the purpose of prosecuting or punishing a person on account of that person's race, religion, nationality, ethnic origin or political opinion or that compliance with the request would cause prejudice to that person's position for any of these reasons.

Article 13

1. A person who is being detained or is serving a sentence in the territory of one State Party whose presence in another State Party is requested for purposes of testimony, identification or otherwise providing assistance in obtaining evidence for the investigation or prosecution of offences under this Convention may be transferred if the following conditions are met:
    (a) The person freely gives his or her informed consent; and
    (b) The competent authorities of both States agree, subject to such conditions as those States may deem appropriate.
2. For the purposes of the present article:
    (a) The State to which the person is transferred shall have the authority and obligation to keep the person transferred in custody, unless otherwise requested or authorized by the State from which the person was transferred;
    (b) The State to which the person is transferred shall without delay implement its obligation to return the person to the custody of the State from which the person was transferred as agreed beforehand, or as otherwise agreed, by the competent authorities of both States;
    (c) The State to which the person is transferred shall not require the State from which the person was transferred to initiate extradition proceedings for the return of the person;
    (d) The person transferred shall receive credit for service of the sentence being served in the State from which he was transferred for time spent in the custody of the State to which he was transferred. 3. Unless the State Party from which a person is to be transferred in accordance with the present article so agrees, that person, whatever his or her nationality, shall not be prosecuted or detained or subjected to any other restriction of his or her personal liberty in the territory of the State to which that person is transferred in respect of acts or convictions anterior to his or her departure from the territory of the State from which such person was transferred.

Article 14

Any person who is taken into custody or regarding whom any other measures are taken or proceedings are carried out pursuant to this Convention shall be guaranteed fair treatment, including enjoyment of all rights and guarantees in conformity with the law of the State in the territory of which that person is present and applicable provisions of international law, including international law of human rights.

Article 15

States Parties shall cooperate in the prevention of the offences set forth in article 2, particularly:

(a) By taking all practicable measures, including, if necessary,adapting their domestic legislation, to prevent and counter preparations in their respective territories for the commission of those offences within or outside their territories, including measures to prohibit in their territories illegal activities of persons, groups and organizations that encourage, instigate, organize, knowingly finance or engage in the perpetration of offences as set forth in article 2;

(b) By exchanging accurate and verified information in accordance with their national law, and coordinating administrative and other measures taken as appropriate to prevent the commission of offences asset forth in article 2;

(c) Where appropriate, through research and development regarding methods of detection of explosives and other harmful substances that can cause death or bodily injury, consultations on the development of standards for marking explosives in order to identify their origin in post-blast investigations, exchange of information on preventive measures, cooperation and transfer of technology, equipment and related materials.

Article 16

The State Party where the alleged offender is prosecuted shall, in accordance with its domestic law or applicable procedures, communicate the final outcome of the proceedings to the Secretary-General of the United Nations, who shall transmit the information to the other States Parties

Article 17

The States Parties shall carry out their obligations under this Convention in a manner consistent with the principles of sovereign equality and territorial integrity of States and that of non-intervention in the domestic affairs of other States.

Article 18

Nothing in this Convention entitles a State Party to undertake in the territory of another State Party the exercise of jurisdiction and performance of functions which are exclusively reserved for the authorities of that other State Party by its domestic law.

Article 19

1. Nothing in this Convention shall affect other rights, obligations and responsibilities of States and individuals under international law, in particular the purposes and principles of the Charter of the United Nations and international humanitarian law.

2. The activities of armed forces during an armed conflict, as those terms are understood under international humanitarian law, which are governed by that law, are not governed by this Convention, and the activities undertaken by military forces of a State in the exercise of their official duties, inasmuch as they are governed by other rules of international law, are not governed by this Convention.

Article 20

1. Any dispute between two or more States Parties concerning the interpretation or application of this Convention which cannot be settled through negotiation

within a reasonable time shall, at the request of one of them, be submitted to arbitration. If, within six months from the date of the request for arbitration, the parties are unable to agree on the organization of the arbitration, any one of those parties may refer the dispute to the International Court of Justice, by application, in conformity with the Statute of the Court.

2. Each State may at the time of signature, ratification, acceptance or approval of this Convention or accession thereto declare that it does not consider itself bound by paragraph 1 of the present article. The other States Parties shall not be bound by paragraph 1 with respect to any State Party which has made such a reservation.

3. Any State which has made a reservation in accordance with paragraph 2of the present article may at any time withdraw that reservation by notification to the Secretary-General of the United Nations.

Article 21

1. This Convention shall be open for signature by all States from 12 January 1998 until 31 December 1999 at United Nations Headquarters in New York.

2. This Convention is subject to ratification, acceptance or approval. The instruments of ratification, acceptance or approval shall be deposited with the Secretary-General of the United Nations.

3. This Convention shall be open to accession by any State. The instruments of accession shall be deposited with the Secretary-General of the United Nations.

Article 22

1. This Convention shall enter into force on the thirtieth day following the date of the deposit of the twenty-second instrument of ratification,acceptance, approval or accession with the Secretary-General of the United Nations.

2. For each State ratifying, accepting, approving or acceding to the Convention after the deposit of the twenty-second instrument of ratification, acceptance, approval or accession, the Convention shall enter into force on the thirtieth day after deposit by such State of its instrument of ratification, acceptance, approval or accession.

Article 23

1. Any State Party may denounce this Convention by written notification to the Secretary-General of the United Nations.

2. Denunciation shall take effect one year following the date on which notification is received by the Secretary-General of the United Nations.

Article 24

The original of this Convention, of which the Arabic, Chinese,English, French, Russian and Spanish texts are equally authentic, shall be deposited with the Secretary-General of the United Nations, who shall send certified copies thereof to all States.

IN WITNESS WHEREOF, the undersigned, being duly authorized thereto by their respective Governments, have signed this Convention, opened for signature at United Nations Headquarters in New York on 12 January 1998.

DOCUMENT No. 14

International Terrorism Conventions

Released by the Office for Counterterrorism
August 17, 1998

There are eleven major multilateral conventions related to states' responsibilities for combating terrorism. This international framework of legal instruments is an important element of U.S. counterterrorism policy. The United States (which has joined all of these conventions) has underscored repeatedly the need for all nations to become party to and implement these existing conventions.

In addition to these conventions, other instruments may be relevant to particular circumstances, such as bilateral extradition treaties, the 1961 Vienna Convention on Diplomatic Relations, and the 1963 Vienna Convention on Consular Relations. Moreover, there are now a number of important United Nations Security Council and General Assembly Resolutions on international terrorism, including three important Security Council resolutions dealing with Libya's conduct in connection with the 1988 sabotage of Pan Am 103, which includes UN Security Council Resolutions 731 (January 21, 1992); 748 (March 31, 1992) and 883 (November 11, 1993).

The following list identifies the major terrorism conventions and provides a brief summary of some of the major terms of each instrument. In addition to the provisions summarized below, most of these conventions provide that parties must establish criminal jurisdiction over offenders (e.g., the state(s) where the offense takes place, or in some cases the state of nationality of the perpetrator or victim).

Terrorism Conventions

1. Convention on Offenses and Certain Other Acts Committed On Board Aircraft (Tokyo Convention, agreed 9/63—safety of aviation):

—applies to acts affecting in-flight safety;

—authorizes the aircraft commander to impose reasonable measures, including restraint, on any person he or she has reason to believe has committed or is about to commit such an act, when necessary to protect the safety of the aircraft and for related reasons;

—requires contracting states to take custody of offenders and to return control of the aircraft to the lawful commander.

2. Convention for the Suppression of Unlawful Seizure of Aircraft (Hague Convention, agreed 12/70—aircraft hijackings):

—makes it an offense for any person on board an aircraft in flight [to] "unlawfully, by force or threat thereof, or any other form of intimidation, [to] seize or exercise control of that aircraft" or to attempt to do so;

—requires parties to the convention to make hijackings punishable by "severe penalties;"

—requires parties that have custody of offenders to either extradite the offender or submit the case for prosecution;

—requires parties to assist each other in connection with criminal proceedings brought under the convention.

3. Convention for the Suppression of Unlawful Acts Against the Safety of Civil Aviation (Montreal Convention, agreed 9/71—applies to acts of aviation sabotage such as bombings aboard aircraft in flight):

—makes it an offense for any person unlawfully and intentionally to perform an act of violence against a person on board an aircraft in flight, if that act is likely to endanger the safety of that aircraft; to place an explosive device on an aircraft; and to attempt such acts or be an accomplice of a person who performs or attempts to perform such acts;

—requires parties to the convention to make offenses punishable by "severe penalties;"

—requires parties that have custody of offenders to either extradite the offender or submit the case for prosecution;

—requires parties to assist each other in connection with criminal proceedings brought under the convention.

4. Convention on the Prevention and Punishment of Crimes Against Internationally Protected Persons (agreed 12/73—protects senior government officials and diplomats):

—defines internationally protected person as a Head of State, a Minister for Foreign Affairs, a representative or official of a state or of an international organization who is entitled to special protection from attack under international law;

—requires each party to criminalize and make punishable "by appropriate penalties which take into account their grave nature," the intentional murder, kidnapping, or other attack upon the person or liberty of an internationally protected person, a violent attack upon the official premises, the private accommodations, or the means of transport of such person; a threat or attempt to commit such an attack; and an act "constituting participation as an accomplice;"

—requires parties that have custody of offenders to either extradite the offender or submit the case for prosecution;

—requires parties to assist each other in connection with criminal proceedings brought under the convention.

5. Convention on the Physical Protection of Nuclear Material (Nuclear Materials Convention, agreed 10/79—combats unlawful taking and use of nuclear material):

—criminalizes the unlawful possession, use, transfer, etc., of nuclear material, the theft of nuclear material, and threats to use nuclear material to cause death or serious injury to any person or substantial property damage;

—requires parties that have custody of offenders to either extradite the offender or submit the case for prosecution;

—requires parties to assist each other in connection with criminal proceedings brought under the convention.

6. International Convention Against the Taking of Hostages (Hostages Convention, agreed 12/79):

—provides that "any person who seizes or detains and threatens to kill, to injure, or to continue to detain another person in order to compel a third party, namely, a State, an international intergovernmental organization, a natural or juridical person, or a group of persons, to do or abstain from doing any act as an explicit or implicit condition for the release of the hostage commits the offense of taking of hostages within the meaning of this Convention;"

—requires parties that have custody of offenders to either extradite the offender or submit the case for prosecution;

—requires parties to assist each other in connection with criminal proceedings brought under the convention.

7. Protocol for the Suppression of Unlawful Acts of Violence at Airports Serving International Civil Aviation (agreed 2/88—extends and supplements Montreal Convention):

—extends the provisions of the Montreal Convention (see No. 3

above) to encompass terrorist acts at airports serving international civil aviation.

8. Convention for the Suppression of Unlawful Acts Against the Safety of Maritime Navigation, (agreed 3/88—applies to terrorist activities on ships):

—establishes a legal regime applicable to acts against international maritime navigation that is similar to the regimes established against international aviation;

—makes it an offense for a person unlawfully and intentionally to seize or exercise control over a ship by force, threat, or intimidation; to perform an act of violence against a person on board a ship if that act is likely to endanger the safe navigation of the ship; to place a destructive device or substance aboard a ship; and other acts against the safety of ships;

—requires parties that have custody of offenders to either extradite the offender or submit the case for prosecution;

—requires parties to assist each other in connection with criminal proceedings brought under the convention.

9. Protocol for the Suppression of Unlawful Acts Against the Safety of Fixed Platforms Located on the Continental Shelf (agreed 3/88—applies to terrorist activities on fixed offshore platforms):

—establishes a legal regime applicable to acts against fixed platforms on the continental shelf that is similar to the regimes established against international aviation;

—requires parties that have custody of offenders to either extradite the offender or submit the case for prosecution;

—requires parties to assist each other in connection with criminal proceedings brought under the protocol.

10. Convention on the Marking of Plastic Explosives for the Purpose of Identification (agreed 3/91—provides for chemical marking to facilitate detection of plastic explosives, e.g., to combat aircraft sabotage):
(Consists of two parts: the Convention itself, and a Technical Annex which is an integral part of the Convention)

—designed to control and limit the used of unmarked and undetectable plastic explosives (negotiated in the aftermath of the Pan Am 103 bombing);

—parties are obligated in their respective territories to ensure effective control over "unmarked" plastic explosive, i.e., those that do not contain one of the detection agents described in the

Technical Annex;

—generally speaking, each party must, among other things: take necessary and effective measures to prohibit and prevent the manufacture of unmarked plastic explosives; take necessary and effective measures to prevent the movement of unmarked plastic explosives into or out of its territory; take necessary measures to exercise strict and effective control over possession and transfer of unmarked explosives made or imported prior to the entry-into-force of the convention; take necessary measures to ensure that all stocks of such unmarked explosives not held by the military or police are destroyed or consumed, marked, or rendered permanently ineffective within three years; take necessary measures to ensure that unmarked plastic explosives held by the military or police, are destroyed or consumed, marked, or rendered permanently ineffective within fifteen years; and, take necessary measures to ensure the destruction, as soon as possible, of any unmarked explosives manufactured after the date-of-entry into force of the convention for that state.

—does not itself create new offenses that would be subject to a prosecution or extradition regime, although all states are required to ensure that provisions are complied within their territories.

11. International Convention for the Suppression of Terrorist Bombing (agreed 12/97—expands the legal framework for international cooperation in the investigation, prosecution, and extradition of persons who engage in terrorist bombings):

—creates a regime of universal jurisdiction over the unlawful and intentional use of explosives and other lethal devices in, into, or against various defined public places with intent to kill or cause serious bodily injury, or with intent to cause extensive destruction of the public place;

—like earlier conventions on protected persons and hostage taking, requires parties to criminalize, under their domestic laws, certain types of criminal offenses, and also requires parties to extradite or submit for prosecution persons accused of committing or aiding in the commission of such offenses.